Villanova Law Student Quotes for
"Short & Happy Guide to Constitutional Law"

Charlie Stegner-Freitag: Dean Alexander is one of those few and fabulous teachers who makes you forget you're in a classroom. By requiring us to look beyond the text of the case itself, to the historical context, the political and social pressures, and comparisons in our current day Dean Alexander gave the plain text of the law *meaning*.

Kyle Platt: The book is immensely helpful in getting a big picture understanding as well as narrowing your focus on cases and material that truly matter. The Dean explains Constitutional Law clearly and with an enthusiasm that is infectious.

Samuel England: Dean Alexander's love for the Constitution permeates his teaching. Whether weaving together Constitutional Law principles or facilitating civil, reasoned debate on controversial legal topics, Dean Alexander made it impossible to leave his course without a healthier respect for the Constitution and our obligation thereto.

Alyssa Pooler: Dean Alexander not only taught the law, but connected it with current events. I believe I am better a lawyer for taking his class.

Nicole Sardella: His passion and enthusiasm for Con Law is contagious. He inspires students to find those connections between course material and current events on their own, both inside and out of the classroom.

Megan Reinprecht: Dean Alexander has a very thorough knowledge of the subject and experience in the field, which he used to illustrate concepts. From the first day of class, we were encouraged to be active participants in the class by bringing in news topics that related to our class, making the law come to life.

Jake Etienne: Thanks to Dean Alexander I've become more involved. He educated me in ways I never had been, inspiring me to take chances I never would have before.

West Academic Publishing's Emeritus Advisory Board

a short & happy guide to

Constitutional Law

Third Edition

Mark C. Alexander
Arthur J. Kania Dean and Professor of Law
Villanova University Charles Widger School of Law

A SHORT & HAPPY GUIDE® SERIES

WEST ACADEMIC

860 Blue Gentian Road, Suite 350
Eagan, MN 55121
1-877-888-1330

Published in the United States of America

ISBN: 979-8-88786-287-3

Acknowledgments

I am so excited to have had the opportunity to write this book. I truly love my job as a law professor, and now as Dean, and this has given me an opportunity to teach countless more students, even if not in my classroom. While writing a book is a complex task, this truly has been a labor of love. And it wouldn't have happened without a whole lot of people helping me along the way.

There are more people than I can mention by name, but I will try my best to say the proper thanks. First, my former colleague at Seton Hall Law, Paula Franzese, introduced me to the good people at West Academic Publishing who came up with the idea of the *Short & Happy* series. She is a model teacher, and a terrific friend. My colleagues at Villanova Law have been wonderfully supportive. Also, thanks to the entire team at West Academic Publishing for making this process enjoyable and productive.

Most thanks go to the teachers who have taught me, and the students I have taught. From grade school, through high school, college, and law school, I am grateful for all the time my teachers have given and the patience that they have shown. For my students, I cannot thank you enough. You give me the gift of your insights and energy. Special thanks to my research assistants along the way, at Seton Hall, Princeton, and now at Villanova. Finally, my best teachers and students are my family, from my sister teaching me to read, to my children teaching me and learning from me every day. My wife, my parents, my children, sister, and my nephews all make me the teacher I am, every day.

Table of Contents

A Short & Happy Guide to Constitutional Law

Third Edition

CHAPTER 1

Welcome and Overview

Welcome to Con Law! For many of you, this is what you've always dreamed of. This is what law school is supposed to be about: big issues, difficult questions, and noble debates. Maybe you even took a class called Constitutional Law in college. But to many others, this is the nightmare of what law school is like: unfamiliar terminology, all full of jargon, extensive history, and convoluted political science, all of which may be new or foreign to you, the Econ, English, or Chemistry major. Well, to all of you I say, throw away your preconceptions, because this class is not what you expected. It is a wonderful course, and it is a hard course. Some of it will feel as familiar as seventh grade civics, and some will feel as foreign as another language. But either way, it is all manageable.

Writing this Short & Happy Guide has been lots of fun. But I also have to say that it has been very challenging. Teaching Con Law is my joy, my passion—I am very lucky to have a job that I love so much. But one thing I love about teaching Con Law is that typically it is not short, and not conducive to being reduced to easy rules. It is very philosophical, and a class where we spend a lot of time **thinking** about the law, and what it ought to be. It contrasts with other classes where every day you are taught clear-cut rules, like

Property and Contracts. More to the point, the various courses in your first year or so are meant to complement each other. Con Law is the place where you spend time in discussion, ask a lot of questions about *why*, and receive fewer concrete rules, frameworks, and three-part tests. You will still get some of that, but the focus is different. So the point is, I find Con Law to be a very **happy** subject, but the discussions aren't always so **short**.

Let me tell you some of the ways and reasons **why** Con Law distinguishes itself, both in law school and here in this book.

The most obvious difference is our starting point, the Constitution of the United States of America. On the first day of class I always give each student a pocket Constitution. In a way, that document is all you need (but not really!). That's all we are interpreting. It's not a statute; it's not the Model Penal Code; it's not the Uniform Commercial Code: it is the charter of existence of our nation, and the basis for this entire class.

But of course, it's 200+ years old, written by a bunch of long-dead white men who lived in a society that was radically different from the one we live in today, in terms of the people, the customs, the language and more. But something about the Constitution endures. It is our beginning point. And inevitably it must be interpreted, in the constant quest "to form a more perfect Union." Perhaps it evolves, as former Justice Stephen Breyer suggests (but a characterization with which the late Justice Antonin Scalia disagreed). Some read it more broadly and others more narrowly. It is at once fluid and static. However we do it, we *read* the Constitution and try to decipher its meaning and application.

Every day in Con Law we discuss the Constitution itself, but also we read Supreme Court decisions. The daily grind of Con Law involves constant reading and re-reading these opinions written over the past 200+ years. These decisions are written by people who have devoted themselves to the exercise of constitutional interpretation, but who don't always agree on the way to carry out that exercise or on the conclusions that exercise elicits. So, as we read casebooks, we see majority opinions. But we also see concurring and dissenting opinions. Sometimes there's not even a majority, so we see a plurality. Only rarely do we read unanimous opinions—there is always a range of ways to answer the questions put before the court. That is all very interesting, but it means that we have few short rules and more long discussions.

So, when I wrote the first edition, I thought to myself, how can I make this *short* and *happy*? The *Happy* is easy—I'm that kind of nerd who truly enjoys reading such opinions; since you are in law school, I'm sure you do too! In terms of the *Short*, I have a basic method for how I present the material. I start with a basic discussion of key principles and cases. But this is not a treatise, hornbook or casebook. I expect that you will be reading your casebook, and you will be taking the time to brief cases, etc. After the discussion of the case, principle, etc., I will ask (and answer), ***What's the takeaway?*** That will be my way of presenting something essential about the case—maybe a three-part test, maybe one clear rule, but maybe something more abstract. And then, I will ask (and answer), ***Why do we read and discuss this?*** That *why* is the meat of Con Law. The cases themselves provide lots of ideas and opinions, and there is rarely one right answer. So, the key thing for you is to know what the various perspectives are as presented in the different opinions; but you also need to know what's really behind it all. What does this case say about the role of the Court, for example; or why do the Justices interpret the Constitution in one manner or another. So, I will ask the *why* question, and I hope that in addition to reading my answer, you will challenge my perspective and also start to think about your own. (And when you are done reading this, let me know what you think—give me your feedback on how to keep it short and happy and *helpful*: email me at dean@law.villanova.edu.)

With that said, let's move forward, and I hope you enjoy this Short & Happy Guide to Constitutional Law.

First, in terms of the substance, there are two major divisions in Con Law: the structural side and the individual rights side. Many schools combine the two into one very big course, like a sort of double-course in one semester, or running over a full year. My discussion, as is typical in most schools, starts with the structural side of Con Law. That will encompass the following broad areas and topics:

- The judicial function in constitutional cases—the who, what, when, where, and why of the Court's role in constitutional adjudication.
- The government's various branches and their powers to regulate national affairs.
- The interaction between the states and the federal system.
- The Commerce Clause, the central source of congressional power.
- Specific provisions of the Constitution that define other powers of the branches of government.
- Separation of powers.

After that, we will look at individual rights, and

- Due Process and Privacy Rights.
- The Equal Protection Clause.

So, let's get started.

CHAPTER 2

The Supreme Court's Authority and Role

A. Judicial Review

We start by discussing the nature and sources of the Supreme Court's authority. This chapter will begin by examining the limitations on the decision-making power of the one court that is most important for our study in Con Law: the United States Supreme Court. It is important to remember that the Supreme Court is very powerful—an unchallenged authority in the country today. But it hasn't always been that way. Now we take a moment to reflect on that underlying assumption, in *Marbury v. Madison* (1803) (Marshall). It is a key case, because it is the foundation for judicial review in America. But it is as tough a first case to read as any, so don't despair—it's tough for everyone. The opinion itself is dense, confusing, and difficult. My job is to help you push through that—in a short and happy kind of way.

There's a very lengthy background to this case, and I will try to cover it concisely. We begin in 1801, when there was great tension between the two reigning political parties—the Federalists (outgoing President Adams) and the Republicans (incoming

President Jefferson). Before leaving office, the Federalists tried to entrench their power and their political philosophy by adding a number of judgeships. Marbury was one of the newly-appointed judges, but his commission was not delivered before Jefferson took office, and as a result Marbury was denied his post. Marbury then sued Madison (who was now in charge of these commissions) to get his commission. Marbury sought a writ of mandamus (a court order compelling a government officer to perform a duty) from the U.S. Supreme Court compelling Madison to deliver the commission. The grounds for Marbury's claims rested on the Judiciary Act of 1789. This act tried to expand the original jurisdiction (basically, where you first file your case—a concept usually covered in Civil Procedure) of the Court and to authorize it to issue writs of mandamus to executive officers, a power not granted to the Court in the Constitution. However, Marbury did not get his writ from the Court. Madison (and therefore Jefferson) won.

The Court ruled against Marbury, holding that it could not issue the writ of mandamus he wanted. More specifically, the Court declared that it lacked jurisdiction to grant mandamus because it did not have original jurisdiction. The Court held the Judiciary Act, which purportedly gave the Court original jurisdiction, to be unconstitutional and therefore void and unenforceable. In getting to its answer, the Court posed and answered three questions to frame the analysis:

1. Did Marbury have a **right** to the commission? Yes. Having been appointed to the position, he had a right to the commission, even if it wasn't delivered in a timely fashion.

2. If he had a right that had been violated, was there a **remedy**? Yes. As a general matter, a right without a remedy is meaningless. In a nation of laws, deprivations of rights of its citizens must be

redressed. In this specific instance, the law (the Judiciary Act of 1789) furnished a remedy for these violations.

3. Was a writ of mandamus from the Court appropriate? **Was this within the Court's power**? The Court said this *could* be a case that called for the writ described by law to be issued. **So the writ may have been the right remedy, but could the U.S. Supreme Court issue it?** No. Marbury got no relief.

What's the takeaway? *Marbury* establishes that **the judicial branch and the Supreme Court have the sole responsibility to weigh the constitutionality of laws.** Marbury had a right that was violated. In our nation of laws, violated rights are remediable. The Judiciary Act authorized the Court to issue writs of mandamus to executive officers. But that law conflicted with the Constitution. What to do with that conflict? The Court responded: **a law which is repugnant to the Constitution is void. It is the Court's duty and power to make such declarations.** No writ.

Why do we read and discuss *Marbury*? *Marbury* sets the foundation for understanding the basic role of the Court going forward in Con Law. The core problem in the case is that Article III, Section 2.2 sets forth a limited set of categories in which the **original jurisdiction** of the Supreme Court may be exercised. In all other cases the Court has **appellate jurisdiction**. *Marbury* is not a case where original jurisdiction is proper, and yet it was not brought pursuant to the Court's appellate jurisdiction. That's a problem, when a statute conflicts with the Constitution. So what happens? The Court voids the statute. This is cleverly done by Chief Justice Marshall, maybe even a genius move.

Before reading *Marbury*, you probably assumed that there was only one way to look at this: a law in violation of the Constitution is not acceptable. Today the term "unconstitutional" is synonymous with *invalid* or *void*. But in the early days of the nation, that proposition had not been established. And that is one of the reasons that this opinion is so difficult to read and understand today. It explores an issue that we consider to be long settled, something that is so much a part of the fabric of our nation that it goes without saying. Because this idea is so fundamental to Constitutional Law, it is easy to overlook that it even had to be discussed at that time. But that is also why this case is so important and why we read and discuss it on the first day of class. We are trying to determine the proper role of the judiciary in our constitutional system, and this case (and course) examines those most fundamental questions.

(Having said that, there's more to discuss. This will still be as short and happy as possible, but just know that this case takes longer than most—but I will reduce it down as much as possible.)

How does the Court decide whether the statute or the Constitution reigns supreme? Chief Justice Marshall clearly established the supremacy of the Constitution and that to hold otherwise would "reduce[ ] to nothing what we have deemed the greatest improvement on political institutions—a written constitution."[1] His conclusion is that—as we all have for so long believed—**a law repugnant to the Constitution is void**. We know that, but stop for a minute. This principle hadn't been established back then, in the earliest days of our nation. So this was really huge.

But that is not the end of the inquiry, and in fact, this is where the most revolutionary part of the opinion kicks in. *Who is to decide whether a law is repugnant to the Constitution, and therefore void?* **The Judicial Branch—found in Article III.** This most-cited part of the whole opinion helps us understand why courts can do this: "*It is emphatically the province and duty of the judicial department to say what the law is.*"[2] You probably thought the answer was obvious

---

1 Marbury v. Madison, 5 U.S. 137, 178 (1803).

2 Id. at 177.

before coming to law school, but it was not so clear 200+ years ago. We are exploring the most fundamental issues of scope of judicial authority under Constitution.

Stop for a moment and ask yourself, *Why?* Seriously. Stop. Ask *Why?*

Do you have an answer yet?

There is no express judicial review provision in the Constitution, so we cannot find a definitive answer there. Instinctively, at least today, it makes sense to us. But the big point here—and why we read and discuss *Marbury* at great length—is that back then, this was all new. We assume it now, so it almost doesn't make sense that we have to read it (which is also why it is a hard case to read). **In the end, *Marbury* declares that the judiciary, or more specifically the U.S. Supreme Court, has the power and the duty of judicial review—to declare laws void.** We read and discuss it at such length to carefully consider this state of affairs, and to lay the foundation for what follows.

Here's one final key point. Chief Justice Marshall could have avoided the question of judicial review in several ways. For example, he could have *recused himself*, given his (and his brother's) intimate involvement with this case. Or, there was an alternate route based on *statutory construction*; Marshall could have read the Judiciary Act differently, to say it merely conferred mandamus power in *appellate* cases. If so, then the proper course would have been to dismiss for lack of jurisdiction, since it was not an appeal. Or he could have read the statute as providing for mandamus as applicable in *original jurisdiction*, which again would have led to dismissal for lack of jurisdiction. A different *common law interpretation* could have changed the decision too, as Marshall could have held that the common law right to a commission vests *upon delivery*, so Marbury had no right to the commission. Or, this could have easily been found to be a *political question* (more on the

Political Question Doctrine coming in the next chapter), out-of-bounds for the judicial branch. One last option to mention: as a matter of *constitutional construction*, Marshall could have read the enumeration of cases in which Court has jurisdiction as a floor, rather than a ceiling. In that case, the expanded authority set forth in the Judiciary Act would have been within congressional power to expand the Court's jurisdiction. However you slice it, using these or other avenues, Chief Justice Marshall could have avoided creating such a big moment.

Given that he could have avoided answering this important question, the question remains: *Why didn't he do so*? Marshall knew he was walking a fine line. If he ruled in favor of Marbury, then President Jefferson likely would have defied the Court order, throwing the young Court into a much weaker position. *This was a **power grab***. At the time, constitutional judicial review was not the norm; it had to be established. In *Marbury*, Chief Justice Marshall found the occasion, establishing judicial review while declaring unconstitutional a statute that arguably increased Court's powers. Politically and practically speaking, Marshall had no choice but to deny Marbury relief. He did more than that. He gave a "victory" on the result to Jefferson and his Republican allies, while strengthening the Court's power as an institution. **Chief Justice Marshall used *Marbury v. Madison* to establish judicial power and to articulate a powerful role for the federal courts—a role that has survived for nearly two centuries.** (That was a lot, but I promise, it gets more short and happy from here going forward!)

Marbury established the Court's power to review the constitutionality of *federal* executive actions and statutes. However, the question of the Court's *authority to review state court decisions* still remained. As we know today, **the U.S. Supreme Court has the ultimate authority to review state court interpretations of the U.S. Constitution**, but that proposition had not been established two centuries ago. *Martin v. Hunter's Lessee* (1810) (Story) established the Court's authority in this area. *Martin* involved two conflicting claims to own land within the state of Virginia. Martin claimed title based on inheritance from Lord Fairfax, a British citizen who apparently had owned the property. On the one hand, the United States and Great Britain had entered into two treaties protecting the rights of British citizens to own land in the U.S. On the other hand, Hunter claimed that Virginia had taken the property before the treaties came into effect, and therefore Martin did not have a valid claim to the land. Resolving the questions depended on the interpretation of a treaty—*a question of federal constitutional law.*

The case was first heard by Virginia courts. The Virginia Court of Appeals ruled in favor of Hunter and, in essence, in favor of the state's authority to have taken the land. The U.S. Supreme Court reviewed and reversed the Virginia court, holding that the federal treaty controlled. In their view, Martin won.

As we think of things today, that Supreme Court ruling should have been the end of it. But here's the problem. In response, the Virginia Court of Appeals declared that the U.S. Supreme Court lacked the authority to review state court decisions. You may be thinking to yourself, *What? State courts can't do that.* Go back 200 years, and it wasn't perfectly clear, which is why this case (like *Marbury*) is hard to fully comprehend the first time through. After the Virginia courts defied the first U.S. Supreme Court ruling, the U.S. Supreme Court again reviewed and **explicitly asserted their power to review state court decisions of federal constitutional questions.**

This point has been subsequently reemphasized a number of times in the Court's history, including from a unanimous Court in the 1958 decision in *Cooper v. Aaron* (Warren). In the immediate aftermath of *Brown v. Board of Education* (1954) (Per Curiam), U.S.

District Courts ordered the desegregation of public schools across the country, including in Little Rock, Arkansas. The state disobeyed that order, in part based on a claim that it was not bound to comply with federal judicial desegregation decrees; they argued that states had the right to determine the meaning of Equal Protection under the U.S. Constitution and that they didn't see that it required integrated schools. Each Justice individually signed the opinion that held: "Article VI makes the Constitution the 'supreme Law of the Land.' [*Marbury*] declared the basic principle that the federal judiciary is supreme in the exposition of the law of the Constitution, and that principle has ever since been respected by this Court and the Country as a permanent and indispensable feature of our constitutional system."[3] This decision stressed the main conclusion from *Martin*, and we can imagine the consequences—what if states didn't have to follow what the U.S. Supreme Court had said in *Brown*?! It is a principle that we have long taken for granted, but it was first established back in *Martin*.

Think about the movies you may have seen about the Civil Rights era, like *Mississippi Burning*, *In the Heat of the Night*, maybe even *Hairspray*. Our nation was in a struggle, in large part with states that opposed integration and a command from society and the courts that society should be integrated. The decisions in these cases make clear that the federal courts' view of the U.S. Constitution (as definitively expressed by the Supreme Court) ultimately trumps—that opinion is the *final* word on the subject.

What's the takeaway? Again we see something that you probably assumed to be true before you started law school. **The U.S. Supreme Court is the final arbiter, the ultimate decision-maker on the U.S. Constitution—it has knowledge and expertise**

---

[3] Cooper v. Aaron, 358 U.S. 1, 18 (1958).

to be. And its word trumps state court interpretations of the U.S. Constitution.

Why do we read and discuss *Martin v. Hunter's Lessee?* It reaffirms the basic power of the Court, and several key points help explain the reasoning in this case:

- **State loyalty.** *State* courts cannot be trusted to adequately protect *federal* rights. State court judges might be more loyal to their state and its constitution, and "state attachments, state prejudices, state jealousies, and state interests might sometimes obstruct, or control, or be supposed to obstruct or control, the regular administration of justice."[4] Or as stated even less delicately in *Cohens v. Virginia* (1821) (Marshall): "In many States the judges are dependent for office and for salary on the will of the legislature."[5]
- **The Supremacy Clause.** The U.S. Constitution is a supreme legal document (Art. VI, cl. 2.) and cannot be subordinated to state charters.
- **Uniformity.** The U.S. Supreme Court's final and exclusive review can ensure uniformity in the interpretation of federal law throughout the nation. Multiple declarations and interpretations only confuse matters

One last quick point on the flip side of the *Martin* coin: There are corresponding limitations on U.S. Supreme Court review of state court decisions. The **U.S. Supreme Court has jurisdiction to review state court determinations of federal law, but not to review state**

[4] Martin v. Hunter's Lessee, 14 U.S. 304, 345 (1816); *see also* U.S. Const. Art. I, § 8, cl. 3.

[5] Cohens v. Virginia, 19 U.S. 264, 386-387 (1821).

court determinations of state law. In *Michigan v. Long* (1983) (O'Connor), the Court emphasized the rule that if *adequate and independent state grounds* exist for a state court ruling, then the U.S. Supreme Court usually will not hear the matter. Our federalist system is built on respect and independence for both the state and federal courts; if the U.S. Supreme Court were to tell state high courts what to do regarding state laws, it would disrespect that division. The Nine in Washington do not have a superior expertise or ability to interpret state constitutions, even if a provision is seemingly identical to one in the U.S. Constitution.

B. Federalism Broadly

The United States of America is not a purely centralized nation-state, nor is it a loose confederation of independent sovereign entities. The Constitution was designed to replace the weak national government of the Articles of Confederation with a stronger federal government, while still maintaining a strong role for states. *Marbury* deals with the *horizontal* relationship between the branches but leaves open the question of the role of courts in determining the *vertical* boundaries between federal and state regulatory power. The horizontal issues explore the interaction between the three branches of government (Legislative, Executive, and Judicial), whereas the vertical relationship concerns the flow of power between the national and the state governments. In a word, we now turn to *Federalism.*

The key case is *McCulloch v. Maryland* (1819) (Marshall). The issue presented concerns whether Maryland could collect a tax from the Bank of the United States. To provide some background, there's a story that spanned over 25 years of fighting between Congress and the Executive Branch over whether Congress had the authority to create the Bank of the United States. This dispute, as in *Marbury,* pitted Federalists, who strongly favored creating the Bank, against

Republicans, who opposed it. Ultimately, Congress created the Bank. After a couple of decades, with the economy in poor health, the Bank attempted to collect on many outstanding loans that were owed by the states. This move by the national government angered many state governments. Some states, including Maryland, reacted by enacting laws prohibiting the national Bank's operation within the state and by imposing significant taxes on the Bank. The Bank in turn refused to pay the tax, so Maryland responded by suing the Bank. In the end, **Chief Justice Marshall construed federal congressional powers broadly and limited the authority of State governments to impede the federal government.**

Chief Justice Marshall considered two questions: First, *Does Congress have the authority to create the Bank?* Yes. Most notably, Marshall observed that **Congress has broad powers pursuant to Article I.** While the Constitution does not enumerate a specific power to create a Bank of the United States, that was not dispositive—it did not resolve the question. The Constitution thus allowed for greater congressional powers, with the opinion observing that while there are some specific enumerated congressional powers, no constitution can describe and anticipate all the possible tools necessary for the job at hand: "In considering this question, then, we must never forget that it is a *constitution* we are expounding."[6] The Court held that *Congress is not limited to those acts specified in the Constitution; Congress may choose any means, not prohibited by the Constitution, to carry out its lawful authority.* If Congress could only do *exactly* that which is stated in the Constitution, paralysis would grip the national government. The Necessary and Proper Clause (Congress has the power "[t]o make all Laws which shall be necessary and proper for carrying into Execution the foregoing Powers, and all other Powers vested by this Constitution in the Government of the United States,

[6] McCulloch v. Maryland, 17 U.S. 316, 407 (1819).

or in any Department or Officer thereof") gave Congress the power to enact the Bank.[7]

The second question was, *is the Maryland tax on the Bank constitutional?* No. This was dispositive. In answering, the opinion staked out powerful territory for the federal government, and consequently, restricted state power. The central premise was that the Constitution controls the laws of the states, and not vice versa.

From this followed three key points:

1. A power to create implies a power to preserve; thus the federal government can create the Bank, and it may take steps to protect it;
2. A power to destroy, if wielded by a different hand, is hostile to, and incompatible with these powers to create and preserve; thus there is a conflict between the federal action and the state's reaction; and
3. Where this repugnancy exists, that authority which is supreme must control and not yield to that over which it is supreme; thus the Bank must stand, and the Maryland tax must fall.

What's the takeaway? Supremacy. The Court struck a strong position in favor of the power of the federal government in holding that the national government is supreme over states. And correspondingly, the Court held that **the states lack authority to negate federal actions**, such as by imposing taxes or regulations on the federal government. The Maryland tax was unconstitutional.

The takeaway in this case really just sets up the question: **Why do we read and discuss *McCulloch?*** First, there's a point about constitutional interpretation. Chief Justice Marshall read the great document **broadly**, so as to effectuate a bigger purpose. And it

---

[7] U.S. Const. art. 1, § 6, cl. 18.

didn't stop there. As with *Marbury,* this case is another **power grab, articulating a broad vision of federal power, specifically increasing the power of the national government** at the expense of the states. Though the Constitution does not enumerate a specific power to create a Bank of the United States, the Court looked more broadly at the meaning behind the document, rather than its explicit enumerations. As Marshall engaged in a close reading of the text of the Articles of Confederation and the Constitution, he focused on very particular points of the use of the term "delegated" to argue for greater congressional powers under the constitutional scheme. Most importantly, he observed that while there are enumerated congressional powers, *no constitution can describe and anticipate all the possible tools necessary for the job at hand.* As noted above, in one of the most famous lines in Con Law, Justice Marshall wrote: "In considering this question, then, we must never forget that it is a *constitution* we are expounding."[8]

Meaning? **The Constitution is fundamentally distinct from and must be read and interpreted differently than a statute.** First, read the Constitution and its goals. Congress should then find the means that best fit those ends. *Congress is not limited to those acts specified in the Constitution; Congress may choose any means not prohibited by the Constitution to carry out its lawful authority.* This is the biggest part of the power grab: expanding the power of Congress. Any limits are found in **the Necessary and Proper Clause** (Art. I, Sec. 8, final clause). The Court holds that **the Bank is constitutional because it was enacted pursuant to congressional authority found in the Necessary and Proper Clause.** So while Congress has room to carry out certain *ends*, there are some limits on the *means* chosen. "Let the end be legitimate, let it be within the scope of the constitution, and all means which are appropriate, which are plainly adapted to that end, which are not prohibited, but

[8] McCulloch, 17 U.S. at 407.

consist with the letter and the spirit of the constitution, are constitutional."[9] And ultimately, Marshall reaffirms *Marbury*: the judiciary can and will review the constitutionality of federal laws, keeping a check on that power.

One last reason why we read and discuss *McCulloch* is to firmly introduce federalism into the course and in particular to weigh some of the advantages of a relatively strong national government, as compared to the advantages of a system of relatively strong state governments.

---

[9] Id. at 422.

CHAPTER 3

Cases and Controversies; Justiciability

A. Standing

In *Marbury* we learned about the power of judicial review, and the wide-ranging nature of Article III courts. But just because the courts have the power to review certain matters does not mean that there are no limits on the exercise of that power. That brings us to fundamental issues of **justiciability.** Justiciability is basically an inquiry into whether a case can be heard by a court. **What does the Constitution say?** Article III, Section 2 reads: "The judicial power shall extend" to "cases" and "controversies." **What does that mean?** Not everything gets heard by federal courts; only cases and controversies.

In order to have a case that can be heard, in order for it to be justiciable, you must have **standing.** The Court has held that there are three basic requirements in order for you to have standing.

1. **Injury-in-fact**

2. **Causation**

3. Redressability

It is constitutionally required that a litigant has suffered (1) **an injury-in-fact** that is (2) **fairly traceable** to the action alleged, and (3) **redressable** by judicial action. There are a couple of cases that help to explain: *Lujan v. Defenders of Wildlife* (1992) (Scalia) and *Massachusetts v. EPA* (2007) (Stevens). Both involve claims about how to protect the environment and natural resources; *Lujan* deals with endangered species, and *Mass. v. EPA* is about global warming and coastal erosion. In each case the Court explained these three main requirements and applied them to the facts, with split results on the big picture of who exactly can bring suit and under what circumstances.

Injury-in-fact. In order to have standing, first, you must have an injury-in-fact. That means that the plaintiff must have suffered a real, concrete harm—the core of Article III concerns for cases and controversies. A plaintiff must show "an invasion of a legally-protected interest which is (a) concrete and particularized, and (b) actual or imminent, not 'conjectural' or 'hypothetical.' "[1] That is a *why* question. This is key to assuring that there is an actual dispute between adverse litigants and to protect against the issuance of advisory opinions. Advisory opinions—usually seeking legal advice in advance of an actual case developing—expand the reach of courts excessively, involving them in matters that may need political resolution, but not court/judicial intervention. A ban on such opinions preserves a proper sphere for the courts—it maintains a clear role for courts in resolving actual cases. Prohibiting advisory opinions also helps to ensure the proper functioning of courts in our system and the proper allocation of resources. The injury-in-fact requirement may also give the parties incentive to litigate thoroughly and effectively, and it ensures that the plaintiff is not

[1] Lujan v. Defenders of Wildlife, 504 U.S. 555, 560 (1992).

an intermeddler, but instead is someone with a real interest of her own to protect.

That's *why*, but what about the specifics? There are two main concerns with implementing the injury requirement: The injury must be (1) *real, imminent* and *not speculative*; and (2) *personal to the plaintiff. Lujan* presented a challenge to changes in the federal regulatory structure surrounding projects overseas, specifically asking what environmental considerations had to be considered under the Endangered Species Act. The plaintiffs, defending their standing, argued that an as yet unplanned future trip to see endangered animals or a vocational interest in studying the animals gave them standing. The *Lujan* Court held that individuals who only had a speculative *interest* in endangered species did not have standing—the plaintiffs failed to show that one of their members would be *directly* affected by the desired application of the Endangered Species Act. This was not found to be an injury because it was neither real nor personal to the plaintiff.

Causation. Injury is necessary, but injury alone is not sufficient. A plaintiff must also allege that the injury is *fairly traceable* to defendant's conduct. This is a concept that we also see in Torts and Criminal Law. Not all actions that might cause an injury are considered proximate, or close enough to be fairly attributable to a defendant. In *Mass. v. EPA*, plaintiffs challenged the EPA over enforcement of the Clean Air Act. Massachusetts and other state and local governments "alleged that the [EPA] ha[d] abdicated its responsibility under the Clean Air Act to regulate the emissions of four greenhouse gases, including carbon dioxide."[2] So the injury-in-fact was alleged to be both global warming, and rising sea levels that erode the coastline. There was no dispute over the causal connection between greenhouse gases and global warming. We all know that many factors cause pollution, and all nations contribute

---

2 Massachusetts v. EPA, 549 U.S. 497, 505 (2007).

to the problem. But was there the appropriate causation on the part of the EPA? The Court said, yes, in effect, every little step can make a difference. Bit by bit the EPA's lack of action *caused* enough injury to Massachusetts for the causation prong to be satisfied.

Redressability. Injury and Causation gets you two-thirds of the way there. The injury-in-fact to the plaintiff that is caused by the defendant must likely be *remedied* if the court rules in favor of the plaintiff. Causation also ties in with redressability, and both are often considered together. But remember that causation is more about liability—who's responsible. Redressability is about the remedy—whether the injury can be fixed. So just finishing off the discussion of *Mass. v. EPA*, the idea is that *if* the EPA were to step up its enforcement, that change could have the constitutionally-required impact. The harm could be redressed by the defendant.

That's some case law. But there's another way to look at it. For a while now, I have read a children's story to my students when we discuss standing. At first it may seem puzzling, even silly, but when we are done you will have a better sense of things. I guarantee you, years afterwards you still remember it. That's been the experience with all my students. What's the story? *The Lorax*, by Dr. Seuss. *Why?* Because there's a recurring theme of protecting natural resources throughout the book. As the story goes, the Once-ler is chopping down Truffula Trees for their soft tufts, to knit a Thneed (while it can be best described as a Seuss-ian Snuggie, the Once-ler claims it's something *everyone* needs). We first see the Lorax the instant after the first Truffula Tree is chopped down. I will skip the dramatic reading, but the Lorax's key line, essentially repeated throughout, is *I speak for the trees, for the trees have no tongues!* And that is what the Lorax does over and over; he speaks and he speaks and he speaks. . . for the trees, the air, the pond, and the creatures that walk, swim and fly; everyone but himself.

As the Once-ler continues chopping down trees, building factories, and making more and more Thneeds, he wreaks havoc on not only the trees, but also on the resident creatures. The destruction of the trees and plants means that the Brown Barbaloots have no food as the trees and plants are destroyed; the Once-ler pollutes the beautiful pond, so the Humming-Fish can't swim; and as the factory fills the air with smog, the Swomee Swans can't breathe and fly. So can the Lorax speak for the trees, and the Brown Barbaloots and the Humming-Fish and the Swomee Swans? In large part, that's a question of **Standing.** Who gets heard?

What's the takeaway from this discussion? First and foremost, we get a three-part test, asking about **(1) injury, (2) causation and (3) redressability**. But as always, there's also layers. One of the key things to note about Standing doctrine is that ironically it gets us involved in the merits of the case. The question involves a preliminary analysis of the facts—can these people bring this suit? So it's seemingly a first-level analysis. But in order to answer this question, the court has to ask about the fundamental merits of a case at the initial pleadings stage, before there's been a significant development of all the facts through discovery. When you read *Lujan* and *Mass. v. EPA*, the split on the Court very much reflects views on the basic subject of environmental protection, and the role of the federal government, as much as the specific three questions asked. *Keep your eye out for that.*

Why do we read and discuss Standing? Because federal courts can't hear any and every grievance that people may have. The Constitution limits courts. And practically speaking, they can't always hear and sort. So realize that the Supreme Court's power is awesome, but it is limited in how it can be exercised. So in that regard, I would advise you to remember that the judicial branch is conservative in many ways. I'm not talking about politics, but there is a conservative nature where the courts just have to wait for the right time, the right person, and the right claim. The justices don't pass laws; they don't execute laws. When there are justiciable claims, then the courts weigh in. But the Standing requirements provide significant limits on how the judicial power is exercised.

B. Mootness and Ripeness

Standing is the clearest doctrinal limit on the basic exercise of Article III judicial power, but there are a couple of other ways in which the courts exercise their discretion in hearing cases that we look at quickly.

Mootness and Ripeness are questions of timing. The question here is *when* is the proper point in time for a matter to be adjudicated? The Constitution has been read to require an *actual controversy* at all stages of federal court proceedings. First, if events subsequent to the filing of a matter resolve the dispute, it should be dismissed as **moot**. But this doctrine is not absolute. When the parties no longer have an interest in the litigation, the case *may* be seen as moot and therefore nonjusticiable. But the doctrine can perhaps be better understood by looking at when it does *not* apply: **a case is *not* moot when the harm to the plaintiff is continuing or when it is capable of being repeated on the plaintiff or others in the future.** Take *Roe v. Wade* as an example, a case you certainly have heard about, even if you haven't yet studied it in class. Ms. Roe became pregnant in 1969. The case was initially brought to court in 1970, and it involved the question of whether this particular pregnant woman had a constitutionally-protected right to choose to terminate pregnancy. After argument and re-argument in the U.S. Supreme Court, three years had passed, and (of course) she was not pregnant. So the actual controversy over whether Ms. Roe had a right to terminate that particular pregnancy was over. But since she (and others) could become pregnant in the future and could again desire to terminate pregnancy, the core legal question was still present, so the case was not moot (See Chapter 7 for a more in-depth analysis of *Roe v. Wade* and subsequent cases in the area).

Ripeness looks at the other end; instead of asking whether the case is over in some sense, it asks whether the controversy has yet begun—*has it ripened to the point where a federal court can review?* The Ripeness doctrine seeks to separate out matters that are premature, such as where injury is speculative, from those cases that are appropriate for review. Ripeness can best be understood as involving the question of when a party may seek pre-enforcement review of a statute or regulation. Customarily, a person can challenge the legality of a statute or regulation only when he or she is prosecuted for violating it. But we cannot require an individual to break a law just to decide whether the law is unconstitutional. It's a Catch-22. Pre-enforcement review walks a fine line, with courts avoiding advisory opinions on matters that don't need judicial input or resolution. Ripeness reflects both constitutional limits and prudential concerns—what is a wise way for the judicial branch to exercise its power. Determining whether a case is ripe requires looking at (1) the hardship on the parties if the court doesn't take up the matter of withholding court consideration and (2) the fitness of the issue for judicial decision. Thus, **in order to be ripe, the plaintiff must allege that she (1) already suffered some harm; (2) is faced with a specific present harm; or (3) is under a threat of specific future harm.**

When it comes to Mootness and Ripeness, think of a legal case as a fine wine. A good wine takes time to age and perfect its taste and flavors. When I was growing up, there was a very popular television commercial featuring Orson Welles (if you're wondering who that is, just ask your parents and they'll tell you). In the ad, Welles delivered the tag line, "We will sell no wine before its time." For its best flavor a wine must mature; at the same time, the wine can sit too long and lose its best qualities. Therefore, a legal case, like a wine, must mature, but cannot wait too long.

What is the takeaway? It's all about timing. You can't bring suit too soon, or too late. You can compare this with Standing, with its focus more on the *type* of injury; Mootness and Ripeness consider *when* the injury and harm occur.

Why do we read and discuss Mootness and Ripeness? It is a very small sliver of Con Law, and mostly helps round out the picture of *when* the courts do (and do not) hear matters. Broadly speaking, it's all about *defining the basic parameters/dimensions of the power of Article III courts.*

C. Political Question Doctrine

The last topic dealing with justiciability is the **Political Question Doctrine.** The articulation of this doctrine has been inconsistent and sometimes confusing. The seminal case is *Baker v. Carr* (1962) (Brennan), which sets forth six factors for deciding whether there is a political question. *Baker* is also an example of the courts expanding their reach generally in a way that had not been done before. Two more recent cases apply this doctrine: *Nixon v. U.S.* (1993) (Rehnquist) and perhaps most famously, *Bush v. Gore* (2000) (Per Curium).

The Political Question Doctrine is grounded in both constitutional and prudential concerns, i.e., based on good judgment or common sense. Constitutionally, it grows out of textual commitment to preserve some decisions for the sole province of the coordinate branches. Prudentially, it is wise for federal courts to avoid political questions to avoid (1) embarrassment of other branches, i.e., conduct of foreign policy; (2) confrontations with other branches; and (3) going where they do not have expertise, thereby preventing judicial over-reaching.

In *Baker v. Carr* we get a set of factors to decide if a matter is a political question or a legal one. A quick bit of background will help first. Tennessee had not changed its apportionment process since 1901; the legislative district boundaries had stayed the same even though the population had moved, grown and shifted significantly over more than half a century. Because of this malapportionment, the voters who brought suit argued that their Equal Protection rights were violated by the debasement or devaluing of their votes. The key question was whether the Court could hear cases alleging this malapportionment. Previously, the Court had stayed out of this issue, because such cases posed political questions.

Justice Brennan wrote for the majority: "Of course the mere fact that the suit seeks protection of a political right does not mean it presents a political question."[3] **So what does that mean?** If it's a legal question, the Court can hear it, but if it's a political question, it cannot. In Chief Justice Marshall's *Marbury* opinion, he instructed that if there is a political question, "nothing can be more perfectly clear than that their acts are only politically examinable. But where a specific duty is assigned by law, and individual rights depend upon the performance of that duty, it seems equally clear that the individual who considers himself injured has a right to resort to the laws of his country for a remedy."[4] As with standing questions, you have to get into the merits and ask: *What is the legal right here*?

Baker v. Carr gave us **six factors to consider when weighing out whether something is a Political Question**:

1. A textually demonstrable constitutional commitment of the issue to a coordinate branch;

[3] Baker v. Carr, 369 U.S. 186, 209 (1962).

[4] Marbury v. Madison, 5 U.S. 137, 166 (1803).

2. A lack of judicially discoverable and manageable standards to decide the case;
3. The impossibility of deciding without making an initial non-judicial policy determination;
4. The impossibility of deciding without showing disrespect for a coordinate branch;
5. An unusual need to adhere to a political decision already made;
6. The potential for embarrassment due to conflicting pronouncements from various branches.[5]

Applying these factors in *Baker v. Carr*, the majority found that there was no political question, so the courts could hear it and resolve the legal question.

Baker v. Carr set the six-factor test you need, and two more recent cases demonstrate its applicability. In *Nixon v. U.S.* federal judge Walter Nixon was convicted of making false statements before a grand jury, in connection with an influence-peddling investigation. Nixon refused to resign from the bench (and he even continued to draw his judicial salary while in prison!). As a result, the House of Representatives adopted articles of impeachment and the Senate, pursuant to its own internal rules, created a committee to hold a hearing and make recommendations to the full Senate. The Committee recommended removal from office and the full Senate voted accordingly. Nixon was impeached and removed from the bench. But he claimed that the Senate's procedure violated Article I, Section 3: "The Senate shall have the sole Power *to try* all Impeachments." He argued that the entire Senate has to *sit and hear* evidence; the use of a committee to hear testimony and make a recommendation was unconstitutional. The Court was not

---

5 Baker v. Carr, 369 U.S. 186, 222 (1962).

persuaded by Judge Nixon's plea, and it decided that the entire issue of proper procedure was in the Senate's hands—*a nonjusticiable political question.* Citing *Baker v. Carr*, the Court held that the Constitution's language and structure demonstrated a textual commitment to Senate.

Finally, some argue that *Baker v. Carr* set the stage for *Bush v. Gore.* I suspect you know the basic facts, so the main point here is that the Court had to decide how ballots should be counted in Florida in the 2000 presidential race. This clearly was a question that was political in nature; it could have been seen as a purely political question for the political branches to sort out. As the Per Curiam opinion stated, "None are more conscious of the vital limits on judicial authority than are the Members of this Court, and none stand more in admiration of the Constitution's design to leave the selection of the President to the people, through their legislatures, and to the political sphere."[6] In essence, if it were a political question the Court would let the Florida process run and stay out of it. But the Court dismissed that concern, instead framing the issue as one of constitutional rights of the candidates (specifically it was framed as an Equal Protection issue). In that light, these were held to be legal, not political questions. It was a question about political things, but not, legally speaking, a political question. Before *Baker v. Carr*, the Court was much less actively involved in questions which were political in nature. But the doctrine defined with greater clarity not only when the courts should stay *out*, but also when they may enter the fray, which they did in *Bush v. Gore*.

What's the takeaway? This takes us back to *Marbury* and the basic idea that the Court should not entertain certain issues, including political questions. This review of the Political Question

---

[6] Bush v. Gore, 531 U.S. 98, 111 (2000) (Rehnquist, C.J., concurring).

Doctrine shows **six factors** and illustrates differing views of Court's proper role and the proper application of these factors.

Why do we read and discuss the Political Question Doctrine? *Baker v. Carr*, and its interpretation of the Political Question Doctrine, opened up the courthouse doors; the Court decided that issues like redistricting plans are justiciable legal questions, and not political questions. Justice Brennan maintained an *expansive view of role of the Court*, to promote and secure individual rights (and the basic principle of one person, one vote). Justice Frankfurter countered with an argument for judicial restraint, concerned that deciding political issues would increase tension between the branches and diminish the Court's stature. In his view, the Court was choosing "among competing theories of political philosophy."[7] That's at the core of this: how far do federal courts reach; when do they assert themselves as protectors of legal rights, versus when do they stay out of decisions that are best left for the political branches. *When is it proper for courts to be involved in cases that are political in nature?* Finally, note the irony in this; while we get six factors to consider, ultimately the court decides whether something is a political question. *The doctrine limits the reach of the courts, but the courts determine the reach of the doctrine.*[8]

---

[7] Baker v. Carr, 369 U.S. 186, 300 (1962) (Frankfurter, J., dissenting).

[8] While these are still relevant inquiries, note that in 2019, the Supreme Court ruled that partisan gerrymandering presents a political question, outside federal court review, even if "incompatible with democratic principles," Rucho v. Common Cause, 588 U.S. 684 (2019).

CHAPTER 4

The Commerce Power

The Commerce Clause is the heart of congressional regulatory power: Article I, Section 8 of the Constitution provides Congress with a broad power "to regulate commerce among the several states."[1] The words may seem simple, but over time, the Court has struggled to define exactly what "commerce" means, and how far it reaches "among the several states." The resolution of these questions often turns on ideological and/or philosophical lines. Ultimately, this issue is about the scope of federal governmental power, and consequently, what is left to the states. Practically speaking, the Commerce Clause provides the authority for a broad range of federal legislation, ranging from criminal statutes to securities regulations to civil rights laws. The Court has used the analysis of these issues to directly consider the scope of congressional powers.

There are three main periods of Commerce Clause analysis:

1. Pre-1937, when the Court grappled with how to define "commerce," and came to a fairly narrow

[1] US Const. art. 1, § 8.

understanding, as the nation moved from an agrarian society to an industrialized nation.

2. 1937–1995, when the Court gave Congress considerable latitude to regulate pursuant to its commerce power.
3. 1995-present, as the Court has reined in congressional power, allowing more room for the states.

We will explore all three periods with most emphasis on the current state of the law.

A. Pre-1937/Early Development

The first glimpse of Commerce Clause interpretation came in *Gibbons v. Ogden* (1824) (Marshall), which basically involved a dispute between two steamboat operators over who was allowed to navigate on which waterways. The key point here is that Chief Justice Marshall held that commerce was not limited to the buying and selling of goods, but broadly extends to cover navigation: "[Commerce] describes the commercial intercourse between nations, and parts of nations, in all its branches. . ." and "among the several states" included local activities "which affect the states generally" or "affect other states."[2]

The Court did not explain too much more about the meaning of the Commerce Clause until the late 19th century. It defined commerce as one stage of business, separate and distinct from other phases like mining and manufacturing and it also made distinctions based on whether things had a direct or indirect impact on commerce. In the first part of the 20th century, the view of the scope of the Commerce power varied, but generally stayed narrow. For example, in *Hammer v. Dagenhart* (1918) (Day), the Court struck

---

2 Gibbons v. Ogden, 22 U.S. 1, 189-190, 195 (1824).

down a child labor law as exceeding congressional power and usurping state power. **Why?** "[Over] interstate transportation, or its incidents, the regulatory power of Congress is ample, but the production of articles, intended for interstate commerce, is a matter of local regulation. . . . If it were otherwise, all manufacture intended for interstate shipment would be brought under federal control. . ."[3] In other words, the child labor law regulated hours and wages in-state, which was beyond the scope of the federal commerce power and reserved for state authority.

The major trend in the pre-1937 period continued with challenges to New Deal programs and illustrated the Court's clear and consistent opposition to an expanded application of the Commerce power. After Franklin Roosevelt was elected during the Great Depression, he took a number of quick steps during his famed first 100 days, pushing many relief measures through Congress, pursuant to its Commerce power. However, the Court responded skeptically in a string of cases in 1935 and 1936, as the Court basically found a fatal *lack of a direct effect on interstate commerce*. Besides an ill-fated court-packing plan, there was enormous pressure to change the direction of constitutional law, as the Court invalidated key provisions of New Deal legislation and cut back on the reach of legislation and congressional powers. The decisions were intellectually vulnerable, because they were based on what could be seen as arbitrary distinctions, such as commerce versus manufacture, or commerce versus production. These distinctions were unsatisfactory to many in that they ignored the obvious effects that the business in question had on commerce—(for example, the refiner of 96 percent of all sugar in the nation was in effect found not to be part of national commerce). Also, some of the opinions were impossible to reconcile; for example, livestock were found to be part of interstate commerce, but chickens were

---

3 Hammer v. Dagenhart, 247 U.S. 251, 272 (1918).

not. The politics and economics of the Great Depression made the Court's attitude even less palatable. In 1937, Justice Roberts changed his position, and the "Switch in time that saved the Nine" signaled change and averted a showdown between the executive and judicial branches. (Then, with seven Supreme Court appointments between 1937 and 1941, FDR got an opportunity to pack the Court after all!)

B. 1937–1995: Shift During the New Deal and After

The next phase overruled earlier decisions and expansively defined the scope of the Commerce power during a nearly 60 year run of Court support of congressional action pursuant to the Commerce Clause. There are four key points.

First, we see **a broader reading of the word "commerce,"** and elimination of technical distinctions in defining the term. For example, *NLRB v. Jones & Laughlin Steel* (1937) (Hughes) was a challenge to the National Labor Relations Act, which created the right of employees to bargain collectively, prohibited practices such as discrimination against union employees, and established the National Labor Relations Board to enforce those provisions. The Court examined the particular facts: Jones & Laughlin was part of a national enterprise, with its Pittsburgh and Aliquippa plants being "the heart of a self-contained, highly integrated body,"[4] employing half a million people in its various enterprises across a number of states. Thus, it seemed simple and easy to declare the business to be about commerce among the several states. But the Court did not limit itself to a ruling on those facts, leaving no doubt that this case marked a major change in the direction of Commerce Clause analysis. The Court spoke broadly about Congress' commerce power: "*The congressional authority to protect interstate*

[4] NLRB v. Jones & Laughlin Steel Corp., 301 U.S. 1, 27 (1937).

commerce from burdens and obstructions is not limited to transactions which can be deemed to be an essential part of a 'flow' of interstate or foreign commerce. . . Although activities may be intrastate in character when separately considered, if they have such a close and substantial relation to interstate commerce that their control is essential or appropriate to protect that commerce from burdens and obstructions, Congress cannot be denied the power to exercise that control."[5]

U.S. v. Darby (1941) (Stone) was a challenge to the constitutionality of the Fair Labor Standards Act of 1938—a law prohibiting the interstate shipment of goods made by employees paid less than the prescribed minimum wage. The Court rejected the argument that regulation of production was left entirely to the states. Instead, Congress may control production by regulating shipments in interstate commerce: "While manufacture is not of itself interstate commerce, the shipment of manufactured goods interstate is such commerce and the prohibition of such shipment by Congress is indubitably a regulation of commerce."[6]

The second point is a **relaxed standard for interpreting "among the several states"** to allow the commerce power to extend from situations where there was only a substantial effect to simply any effect on interstate commerce, or even solely a rational basis for congressional action.

That directly relates to the third major point from this era: the Court demonstrated **significant deference to Congress**. As in each major case, the Court let Congress regulate without much challenge from the judiciary. For example, in two cases dealing with the Civil Rights Act of 1964, the Court upheld the legislation, in large part deferring to congressional findings that the reach of the hotel and

5 Id. at 36-7 (emphasis added).

6 United States v. Darby, 312 U.S. 100, 113 (1941). Note also that this decision overruled *Hammer*.

restaurant industries across the country affects commerce among the several states. (*See Katzenbach v. McClung* (1964) (Clark); *Heart of Atlanta Motel v. U.S.* (1964) (Clark).)

Fourth, there is a **diminution of the role and power of the Tenth Amendment.** The Court in *Darby* wrote that the Tenth Amendment "states but a truism that all is retained which has not been surrendered."[7] In other words, the Tenth Amendment would not be used by Court as a basis for invalidating federal laws, and a law is constitutional so long as it is within the scope of Congress' power. Federal power was on the rise, and state power was on the decline.

Those four points are significant thematically, particularly as a set-up for the final, current state of Commerce Clause analysis.

C. Post-1995: Rehnquist Court's Revival of Internal Limits

Everything changed in 1995, with *U.S. v. Lopez* (Rehnquist). Alfonso Lopez, a 12th grader at Edison High School in San Antonio, was arrested for carrying a concealed .38 caliber handgun and five bullets. He was charged with violating a federal law, the Gun-Free School Zones Act of 1990, making it an offense "knowingly to possess a firearm at a place that the individual knows . . . is a school zone."[8] The Court held that Congress exceeded its Commerce Clause power in enacting the Gun-Free School Zones Act. The Court held that there are three categories of activities that Congress can regulate under its Commerce power:

1. **Congress can "regulate the use of the channels of interstate commerce."**

---

7 Id. at 124.

8 United States v. Lopez, 514 U.S. 549, 551 (1995).

2. **Congress can "regulate and protect the instrumentalities of interstate commerce, or persons or things in interstate commerce."**
3. **Congress may "regulate those [*intra*state] activities having a *substantial relation to inter*state commerce."[9]**

The Court made several key points which you should note. (Plus, here's just a little tip: if you pull up the full opinion, Chief Justice Rehnquist provides long introductory remarks that trace the history of Commerce Clause jurisprudence, almost like a hornbook.) First, the opinion reviewed prior case law that suggested a virtually unlimited range of intrastate activity (activity *within* individual states) that may be regulated under the substantial effects test. The prior case law suggested a much more significant connection between the regulated *intra*state activity and the *inter*state economic activity that can be regulated than the activities present in *Lopez*. That looser connection was problematic. The second major flaw was that the Act "contains no jurisdictional element which would ensure, through a case-by-case inquiry, that the firearm possession in question affects interstate commerce."[10] Third, the Court rejected the federal government's claim that the Act could be justified under the Commerce Clause because possession of a gun near a school may result in violent crime that can ultimately adversely affect the economy. In other words, the Court rejected a sort of rational basis review. Finally, the Court emphasized that there is a distinction between "What is truly national and what is truly local."[11] It is difficult line-drawing, but it is possible, and required, to stay true to the Constitution.

---

9 Id. at 558-59.

10 Id. at 562.

11 Id. at 567-8.

It's also worth noting that Justice Thomas concurred, urging an even narrower view of congressional authority than adopted by majority. "I write separately to observe that our case law has drifted far from the original understanding of the Commerce Clause. In a future case, we ought to temper our Commerce Clause jurisprudence in a manner that both makes sense of our more recent case law and is more faithful to the original understanding of that Clause."[12] Thomas's argument stems from his interpretation of the text, structure, and history of the Commerce Clause. His approach (which could be labeled originalist, textualist, or strict constructionist) would have returned the Court to the 1887–1937 position, when it disallowed virtually all attempts of Congress to regulate pursuant to the Commerce Clause.

What's the takeaway? First and foremost, Rehnquist established three things to look for in doing Commerce Clause analysis: (1) channels; (2) instrumentalities; or (3) a substantial relation to interstate commerce. More broadly, this is a revival of a **narrower reading of the commerce power and a more serious balancing of state and federal interests** that had been relaxed during the long era of judicial deference to Congress. The substantial effects test now has serious bite and may invalidate laws previously thought to be within congressional power.

Lopez is highly significant because it marked the first time in 60 years that a federal law was declared unconstitutional as exceeding the scope of Congress' commerce power. However, it left open many questions about (1) how far Congress can go in protecting the channels of commerce; (2) what is a "substantial effect" on interstate commerce; and (3) how much deference is to be granted to congressional action.

---

[12] Id. at 584 (Thomas, J., concurring).

The Court gave a potentially conflicting answer in *Gonzales v. Raich* (2005) (Stevens), as it upheld the broad federal power to regulate marijuana, effectively trumping states and localities, and specifically invoking *Wickard v. Filburn* (1942) (Jackson), a quintessential case at the height of the period of Court deference to the expansive power of the Congress under the Commerce Clause. The Court staked no *new* territory in *Raich*, but it was noticeably more deferential to the Congress and less so toward the states, contrary to the direction in *Lopez* and other modern decisions.

Moving forward in time, note that the Court did *not* rely on the Commerce Clause in its closely-watched opinion to uphold the individual mandate in the Affordable Care Act, *National Federation of Independent Business v. Sebelius* (2012) (Roberts), which we will talk about more in Chapter 6. The Court held that the Congress could not rely on its commerce power to require individuals to buy into the health insurance market, if they are not already in it. "The power to *regulate* commerce presupposes the existence of commercial activity to be regulated. . . . The language of the Constitution reflects the natural understanding that the power to regulate assumes there is already something to be regulated."[13] While other Justices concurred in the result, this part of the opinion drew dissent, as an improper restraint on the commerce power that will not endure.

Why do we read and discuss the Commerce Clause cases, and especially *Lopez*? *Lopez*, and all Commerce Clause cases, raise several broader ideas you need to grapple with.

1. **Sport.** There's an argument that the only problem with the Gun Free School Zones Act was bad drafting by Congress, which failed to put in a jurisdictional requirement that a gun had *moved in interstate*

---

[13] NFIB v. Sebelius, 567 U.S. 519, 550 (2012).

commerce. Congress could (and did) easily cure this defect by adding this requirement into the law. So, it's all about the **sport** of Congress adhering to parameters that have now been more clearly defined by the Court. It's like two boxers going back and forth at each other—one jabbing and the other ducking but coming back with an uppercut. Maybe it's like the *Rocky* series of movies. Rocky is down, then up: he wins, he loses. One fight goes to Rocky, the next to Apollo Creed, Clubber Lang or Ivan Drago, then back to Rocky, etc. The point is, there is a constant back and forth, with two well-matched contestants trying to establish their own power.

2. **State autonomy.** The opinion written by Chief Justice Rehnquist favors robust protection of state autonomy, and he emphasizes that this law encroaches into an area where states have historically been sovereign (like family law, criminal law, and education). **Thus the modern reading of the commerce power empowers the States and limits the federal government.**

3. **Power grab.** Chief Justice Rehnquist reached out with the power of the Court to limit the power of the U.S. Congress. According to Rehnquist, Congress was out of control, and he flexed judicial muscle to reign in a coordinate branch of government. (The side effect of empowering states is not a bad thing either, from Chief Justice Rehnquist's perspective.)

D. Tenth and Eleventh Amendment Limitations

Finally, there are two other limits on federal power, and a corresponding protection of states' power that connect with the Commerce Clause.

The Tenth Amendment provides "The powers not delegated to the United States by the Constitution, nor prohibited by it to the States, are reserved to the States respectively, or to the people."[14] So what does that mean? The Tenth Amendment limits congressional power to regulate commerce in a different way than the Commerce Clause does. It applies because congressional actions can have the effect of impeding and imposing upon the States.

Remember that in *Darby,* the Court said that the "Tenth Amendment states but a truism that all is retained which has not been surrendered."[15] From then (1941) through 1992, the Court consistently endorsed the perspective that a law is constitutional so long as it is within the scope of congressional power, i.e., *the Tenth Amendment was not to be a basis for invalidating federal laws.* Then came Justice O'Connor's opinion in *New York v. U.S.* (1992). In 1985, the Low-Level Radioactive Waste Act created a statutory duty for states to provide for safe disposal of radioactive waste generated within their borders. Part of the law required states to take title to any wastes within their borders that were not properly disposed of and then to be liable for all damages directly or indirectly incurred. While Congress had the authority to regulate disposal of radioactive waste, so too could states; thus a clash of interests and authority. Within the law, there were monetary incentives for the states to comply, which were found to be permissible, but the "Take Title" provision, which gave state governments a choice between accepting ownership of waste or

[14] US Const. amend. X.

[15] United States v. Darby, 312 U.S. 100, 124 (1941).

regulating according to Congress' instructions, was held unconstitutional. "A choice between two unconstitutionally coercive regulatory techniques is no choice at all."[16] Forcing states to accept ownership of radioactive waste would *impermissibly "commandeer" state governments*. Allowing Congress to commandeer state governments would undermine government accountability, because the U.S. Congress could make a decision, but the states would take the political heat and be responsible for a decision that was not theirs. Similarly, requiring state compliance with federal regulatory statutes would improperly impose on a state's choice. Congress *cannot compel states to administer a federal regulatory program*.

Printz v. U.S. (1997) (Scalia) is another case where the Tenth Amendment provided an affirmative limit on the federal power. It involved the Brady Act, which regulates firearms sales: One part of the original law enlisted local law enforcement officers (like Sheriff Printz of Ravalli County, MT) to assist in the background-checking of would-be gun purchasers. Printz objected, arguing that he was a *state* official being improperly drafted to enforce *federal* legislation. As the majority wrote, he "object[ed] to being pressed into federal service, and contend[ed] that congressional action compelling state officers to execute federal laws is unconstitutional."[17] The Court invalidated the portion of Brady Act that required local sheriffs to make reasonable efforts to perform background checks on handgun purchasers because, as Justice Scalia wrote for the majority, "The Federal Government may neither issue directives requiring the States to address particular problems, nor command the States' officers, or those of their political subdivisions, to administer or enforce a federal regulatory program. It matters not whether policymaking is involved, and no case-by-

[16] New York v. United States, 505 U.S. 144, 176 (1992).

[17] Printz v. United States, 521 U.S. 898, 905 (1997).

case weighing of the burdens or benefits is necessary; such commands are fundamentally incompatible with our constitutional system of dual sovereignty."[18]

What is the takeaway? After *New York v. U.S.* and *Printz*, the Tenth Amendment provides a basis to challenge federal laws that force state administrative or legislative action, such as energy and environmental laws. *If a federal law (commandeers the state government or) compels state legislative or regulatory activity, the statute will be found unconstitutional, even if there is a compelling need for the federal action.* (As we will see soon in Chapter 6, while it is unconstitutional for Congress to compel state legislatures to adopt laws or to force state agencies to adopt regulations, Congress is not powerless. Congress may set standards that state and local governments must meet and thereby *preempt* state and local actions. Congress may attach strings on grants to state and local governments, and through conditions induce state/local actions that it cannot directly compel.)

In a recent application of these principles, *Murphy v. NCAA* (2018) (Alito)[19] confirms and applies *New York v. U.S.*, in the context of the power of the states to regulate gambling on sports. More specifically, the Court held that a federal statute prohibiting the modification or repeal of state-law prohibitions on sports gambling impermissibly commandeered the regulatory power of states in contravention of *New York v. U.S.*

Why do we read and discuss the Tenth Amendment? We get a greater sense of the current movement to re-assert states' rights and to restrain the power of the federal government. Look at this not just as Tenth Amendment cases, but also look at the time span—a five-year span with *New York v. U.S.* in 1992, *Lopez* three years later, and *Printz* in 1997. In a short period of constitutional history,

---

[18] Id. at 935.

[19] Murphy v. NCAA, 584 U.S. 453 (2018).

the Court's federalism concerns serve as the basis to constrain federal congressional actions and powers. As Scalia wrote in *Printz*, "The Framers rejected the concept of a central government that would act upon and through the States [as had the Articles of Confederation], and instead designed a system in which the state and federal governments would exercise concurrent authority over the people."[20]

Finally, a quick word about the **Eleventh Amendment.** The text reads: "The Judicial power of the United States shall not be construed to extend to any suit in law or equity, commenced or prosecuted against one of the United States by citizens of another state."[21] It limits the power of the federal courts over the states and can be seen as part of the federalism revival, with one key case coming in that same five-year span I just mentioned. In *Seminole Tribe v. Florida* (1996) (Rehnquist) the Court held that Congress cannot override the Eleventh Amendment pursuant to the Commerce Clause power. *Congress cannot abrogate the state's Eleventh Amendment sovereign immunity. The Eleventh Amendment creates an important limit on federal court jurisdiction, prohibiting suit in federal court against state governments by any private person.*

---

[20] Printz v. United States, 521 U.S. 898, 919-20.

[21] US Const. amend. XI.

CHAPTER 5

The Dormant Commerce Clause

The Dormant Commerce Clause keeps interstate commerce free from state or local interference. State and local laws are unconstitutional if they place an *undue burden on interstate commerce*. While there is *no specific constitutional provision* that expressly declares that the states may not burden interstate commerce, it is doctrine *inferred from* the grant of the power directly to Congress to regulate commerce among the several states. *When Congress has legislated in the area*, federal law may preempt state or local law. But with no pre-existing federal law or preemption, state or local law can be challenged on the ground that *it excessively burdens commerce among the states.* **Even if/when Congress has not acted to regulate—that is, when its commerce power lies dormant—state and local laws can still be challenged as unduly interfering with interstate commerce.**

There are several reasons for Dormant Commerce Clause analysis. As a **historical** matter, as the Framers were building a nation, there is evidence that they intended to prevent protectionist state laws that would interfere with interstate commerce. In terms of **economic theory,** the reason for that scheme is that the national economy is better off if state and local laws impeding the flow of interstate commerce are stricken. If one state acts to help itself at the expense of the others, the other states are likely to retaliate with their own protectionist schemes, ultimately stifling production and harming the national economy. That hurts all, in every state. As a **political** matter, the argument goes, states and their citizens should not be harmed by laws in other states where they lack political representation. These themes and justifications are more complementary than exclusive, all emphasizing the overarching point that *states should not be able to obstruct interstate commerce, and no one state should be able to discriminate against products, manufacturers, shippers etc. from out-of-state.*

The doctrine's origins can be found in *Gibbons v. Ogden* (1824) (Marshall), which, as we saw briefly before, was a dispute over local laws regulating commercial navigation on rivers. The Court explained: "when a State proceeds to regulate commerce. . . among the several states, it is exercising the very power that is granted to Congress, and is doing the very thing which Congress is authorized to do."[1] The natural implication of this statement is that *Congress' commerce power is exclusive, and state regulation of interstate commerce is inconsistent with that federal power.* Thus the doctrinal point has followed that *the federal power to regulate commerce includes the (negative) power that states should **not** be able to regulate commerce in a way that interferes with the federal congressional prerogative to regulate.*

From those simple beginnings, much has followed. Modern Dormant Commerce Clause analysis turns heavily on the distinction between *discriminatory purpose and effect,* and the *discriminatory impact* of state laws on commerce. Also, questions of *level of*

---

1 Gibbons v. Ogden, 22 U.S. 1, 199-200 (1824).

scrutiny are raised, as well as questions of *balancing*. Three basic concepts emerge:

1. Laws that are **facially discriminatory** against out-of-state commerce are subject to the **strictest scrutiny**; such laws are virtually per se invalid (they must be necessary to achieve an important purpose).
2. Laws that are **facially neutral but clearly protectionist** in purpose or effect also will typically be stricken **as impermissibly burdening** interstate commerce.
3. Those statutes that simply have a **disproportionately adverse impact** on interstate commerce are subject to **intermediate scrutiny**—such as the *Pike* balancing test (laws will be invalid if their burdens on interstate commerce outweigh the benefits to the state).

A. Facially Discriminatory Statutes

Laws that are facially discriminatory against out-of-state commerce are subject to strictest scrutiny—they are virtually per se invalid (necessary to achieve an important purpose). Cases reflect a basic principle that outright facial discrimination by one state or local government against another is unconstitutional. For example, in *Philadelphia v. New Jersey* (1978) (Stewart) the Court struck down a New Jersey law that prohibited waste importation from outside the state. The garbage in question was seen as an object of commerce, and while states may regulate commerce in the absence of federal regulation, the question was, *What are the limits on such regulation?* The Court said: "Where simple economic protectionism is effected by state legislation, a virtually *per se* rule of invalidity has been erected."[2] There were different possible explanations for the law, but the Court wrote, "whatever New Jersey's ultimate purpose, it may not be accomplished by discriminating against articles of commerce coming from outside the state unless there is some reason, apart from their origin, to treat them differently."[3]

If the law is not one of simple economic protectionism, but instead regulates in an evenhanded manner to promote a legitimate local public interest, then *are the interstate commerce effects of the state statute incidental*? If not, the law is unconstitutional, because, as found in this case, "The New Jersey law at issue in this case falls squarely within the area that the Commerce Clause puts off limits to state regulation."[4]

In *Dean Milk Co. v. Madison* (1951) (Clark), we see another example of a facially discriminatory statute, this time in a challenge to a local ordinance that barred the sale of pasteurized milk unless processed and bottled at approved plants within five miles of Madison, Wisconsin. Dean Milk, based in Illinois, was denied a permit to sell solely because its plants were 65 and 85 miles away from Madison, even though it used federally recommended standards, otherwise suggesting its milk was fit to be sold there. While the avowed **purpose of the ordinance** was to protect the health and safety of the people of Madison, the Court deemed it **protectionism**. The law advantaged businesses in or near the city at the expense of other businesses, and additionally there appeared to have been alternative means available to serve Madison's avowed goals. Speaking to the broader theme at the end of the opinion, this passage typifies Dormant Commerce Clause analysis: "To permit Madison to adopt a regulation not essential for the protection of

---

2 City of Philadelphia v. New Jersey, 437 U.S. 617, 624 (1978).

3 Id. at 626-27.

4 Id. at 628.

local health interests and placing a discriminatory burden on interstate commerce would invite a multiplication of preferential trade areas destructive of the very purpose of the Commerce Clause."[5]

What's the takeaway? These laws were invalid because they erected barriers to the free flow of interstate commerce in an area where Congress had not acted. Likewise, in *Carbone v. Clarkstown* (1994) (Kennedy), the Court wrote: "Discrimination against interstate commerce in favor of local business or investment is *per se* invalid, save in a narrow class of cases in which the municipality can demonstrate, under rigorous scrutiny, that it has no other means to advance a legitimate local interest."[6] *If a law is facially discriminatory, it is presumed to be invalid.* But just because a state law is facially discriminatory, it is not *automatically* invalid; it is *subject to strict scrutiny/virtually per se invalid*, a rebuttable presumption. If a facially discriminatory measure serves a legitimate local purpose that could not be served by *any other* non-discriminatory measures, it may survive judicial review.

Why do we read and discuss this? It starts us off with the basic rule that states cannot interfere with interstate commerce in order to serve protectionist goals. "What is crucial is the attempt by one state to isolate itself from a problem common to many by erecting a barrier against the movement of interstate trade."[7] And it also gives us the broader theme, as expressed in the end of the *Philadelphia v. New Jersey* opinion, that while this ruling protects New Jersey's neighbors today, it protects New Jersey tomorrow. "The Commerce Clause will protect New Jersey in the future, just as it protects her neighbors now, from efforts by one State to isolate itself in the stream of interstate commerce from a problem shared

[5] Dean Milk Co. v. City of Madison, 340 U.S. 349, 356 (1951).

[6] C & A Carbone v. Town of Clarkstown, 511 U.S. 383, 392 (1994).

[7] City of Philadelphia v. New Jersey, 437 U.S. 617, 628 (1978).

by all."[8] There's a "what-goes-around-comes-around" argument that hinges on the concern over the consequence of the nation's future if the Court had decided otherwise. So in this sense, the **Dormant Commerce Clause serves to prevent trade wars among the states.**

Imagine an old-fashioned string of Christmas lights. If any one light is pulled off, it can cut the rest of the lights along the string, and the whole tree looks sort of bad. Or maybe it's a hose being pinched. If the flow runs unimpeded, the entire garden can be watered effectively. But when you pinch off part, the flow is slowed, with negative consequences. The Dormant Commerce Clause analysis has at its core a concern for a free flow of goods across the United States, which the Commerce Clause reserves for federal congressional regulation. And the states should not interfere.

B. Facially Neutral, Protectionist Purpose

Unlike the laws we saw in *Philadelphia v. NJ* and *Dean Milk*, many laws might not reflect a clearly stated intent to exclude outsiders, but *if the Court finds a discriminatory purpose and/or effect, it will strike down the state/local regulation. Laws that are facially neutral but clearly protectionist in purpose or effect will typically be stricken as impermissibly burdening interstate commerce.* The Court has found facially neutral state and local laws to be unconstitutionally discriminatory based on their purpose and/or effect, based on the idea of one nation, one economy. The states are a part of that whole economic unit that can work cooperatively, albeit sometimes at an individual state's expense.

Baldwin v. Seelig (1935) (Cardozo) provides one example where there were impermissible state-imposed barriers to out-of-

---

[8] City of Philadelphia v. New Jersey, 437 U.S. 617, 629 (1978).

state sellers. A New York act set minimum prices for New York dealers to pay New York milk producers; it also prohibited the sale of out-of-state milk purchased below the set New York purchase price. Seelig (from Vermont) argued this was improper economic isolationism, a state-created barrier to incoming trade that hindered access to markets. The Court held that the New York regulation set a barrier as effective as a straight customs duty; and if New York could do it, then any state could. Most notably, the Court offered this vision of a national economy: "The Constitution was framed under the dominion of a political philosophy less parochial in range. It was framed upon the theory that the peoples of the several states must sink or swim together, and that in the long run prosperity and salvation are in union and not division."[9] Thus no single state can unduly interfere with that theory of *nation*, and this law was stricken.

Just as it is improper to prohibit out-of-staters from *buying in state*, when states try to prohibit out-of-staters from purchasing a state resource and *taking it out-of-state*, that raises additional, different Dormant Commerce Clause problems. For example, in *H.P. Hood & Sons v. DuMond* (1949) (Jackson), a Boston milk distributor obtained milk from New York producers and maintained three receiving depots in New York. He wanted a fourth, but was rejected, pursuant to a New York law stating that no new licenses would be issued unless issuance would not tend to be destructive to competition. The new depot would shorten delivery routes and divert milk from other buyers. The issue then became whether New York could deny additional facilities in order to protect and advance local economic interests. While New York tried to justify this regulation of commerce as an attempt to ensure fair prices and sanitary milk, the Court said the real purpose was rather blatant: *to aid the local economy, at the expense of out-of-state commerce.*

---

[9] Baldwin v. G.A.F. Seelig, Inc., 294 U.S. 511, 523 (1935).

The opinion echoed major themes of Dormant Commerce Clause analysis: (1) respect for state power to regulate in certain areas; (2) rejection of states curtailing commerce; (3) recognition that the economic unit is the nation; (4) prevention of economic isolation—the danger of each state having individual barriers. There is a *distinction between protecting health and safety, when related to interstate commerce, and constricting the flow of commerce for economic advantage. The former is tolerated; the latter is not.*

What's the takeaway? Laws that are protectionist in purpose, even though facially neutral, will be found to violate the Dormant Commerce Clause. In this nation, the economic unit cannot survive with fifty states imposing fifty barriers to the free flow of trade. As the *Baldwin* Court wrote: "What is ultimate is the principle that one state in its dealings with another may not place itself in a position of economic isolation."[10]

Why do we read and discuss these cases? As the Court moves out of the examination of whether a law is discriminatory on its face, it seeks to discern whether there is a *protectionist purpose*. That inquiry reveals greater insight into the purposes behind the Dormant Commerce Clause doctrine. Remember, the commerce power lies dormant, so the question is whether the state/local law interferes *not* with a specific federal enactment, but whether it interferes with a broader notion of the free flow of commerce among the several states. And in trying to answer that question, we start to see questions of *how* a court is capable of making such a determination. The Court is making more inferences, expressly considering questions of the philosophy of our governmental system, as it combines nation and states.

It's like a moving pick in basketball. If you already establish your position, that's okay. Nobody has the right to do anything

---

[10] Id. at 527.

anywhere, and there are legitimate barriers to movement on the basketball court. But when you slide into it, maybe throw your hip into the other player, the ref blows the whistle and calls a foul. So when a state throws up an improper barrier to trade among the states, with the clear intent to impede the flow of commerce, the courts step in and call a foul, applying Dormant Commerce Clause principles.

C. Facially Neutral, Disproportionate Adverse Effect

The largest group of Dormant Commerce Clause cases involves transportation—regulating trucks and trains—and these cases typically contain laws that are facially neutral but have a significant negative effect on interstate commerce. In this last group of cases, the general rule is that *facially neutral statutes that have a disproportionately adverse impact on interstate commerce are subject to a lower level of review—intermediate scrutiny—using the* Pike *balancing test. In doing that balancing, the question is whether the burdens outweigh the benefits.*

In *Pike v. Bruce Church, Inc.* (1970) (Stewart), the Court held: "Where the statute regulates even-handedly to effectuate a legitimate local public interest, and its effects on interstate commerce are only incidental, it will be upheld unless the burden imposed on such commerce is clearly excessive in relation to the putative local benefits."[11] So the key analytical question is: *Do the burdens on interstate commerce outweigh the benefits to the regulating state?* This is the *Pike* balancing test that applies to facially neutral laws.

For example, in *Kassel v. Consolidated Freight* (1981) (Powell) the Court reviewed an Iowa law restricting the use of 65-foot double

[11] Pike v. Bruce Church, Inc., 397 U.S. 137, 142 (1970).

trailer trucks, supposedly because they were more dangerous than 55-foot singles. As a result, many trucking companies could not drive their trucks through Iowa, and that necessitated detours that caused costs to rise significantly. For several reasons, the Court struck down the law, finding (1) as an empirical matter, doubles are as safe as singles; (2) other states in the region did not have similar laws; (3) the joint impact of (1) and (2) was a great economic burden on trucking companies and interstate commerce; and (4) a special exemption in the statute and protectionist language used by government officials suggested that Iowa was motivated by protectionist desires, not public/road safety. The key point is that the Court weighed the benefits against the burdens—*Pike* balancing—and found the law to be unconstitutional.

The Court recently discussed *Pike* in *National Pork Producers Council v. Ross* (2023) (Gorsuch). There, the plurality engaged in *Pike* balancing, while acknowledging the challenges of such judicial analysis, but still *Pike*'s "clearly excessive" requirement remains.

What's the takeaway? *Dormant Commerce Clause analysis of facially neutral statutes requires the* Pike *balancing test, which weighs the benefits of the statute against the burdens it imposes on interstate commerce.*

Why do we read and discuss this? This is the last part of the three major aspects of Dormant Commerce Clause analysis. Beyond the core issue of the importance of a national economy and states not interfering with the free flow of commerce, *Pike* balancing calls into question the basic role and competency of courts. Because *Pike* balancing is highly fact-sensitive, a reviewing court has to insert itself into the details and perform a sort of policy analysis—benefits vs. burdens—and assert its expertise as judges weighing competing arguments in light of the facts presented. Some argue that this is a job best left to legislatures, while others argue that the courts can do the job better.

At the end of this three-part discussion on the Dormant Commerce Clause, I ask one last time: *What's the takeaway?* *The first question is: does a law discriminate against out-of-staters or does it treat all alike?* (1) *Laws that facially discriminate against out-of-staters are virtually* per se *invalid and will be upheld only if they survive the strictest scrutiny.* (2) *Laws that are facially neutral but clearly protectionist in purpose or effect also will typically be stricken as impermissibly burdening interstate commerce.* (3) *Those statutes that simply have a disproportionately adverse impact on interstate commerce are subject to a sort of intermediate scrutiny in the* Pike *balancing test, in which a court weighs burdens against benefits.*

One last pair of analogies that might help: you might think of Dormant Commerce Cause power as akin to the power of a dormant volcano. A volcano will lie inactive until certain geological conditions come together to activate the volcano, eventually forcing it to erupt. The federal dormant commerce power lies inactive until certain conditions cause it to activate, with those being the condition of state and local regulation of commerce. When the conditions are right and commerce is impeded, the volcano can erupt and effectively wipe out the state regulations that were improperly imposed. Or consider the analogy of crabs in a barrel: if each state, like a crab in a barrel, never lets any other state rise up, then none survive. The cut-throat competition among the states, like that of the crabs in the barrel, ultimately dooms all.

D. Privileges and Immunities Clause

The Privileges and Immunities Clause provides another limitation on the powers and actions of states. (Art. IV, Sec. 2: "The Citizens of each state shall be entitled to all Privileges and Immunities of Citizens in the several states."[12]) *It limits the ability*

[12] US Const. art. IV, § 2.

of one state to discriminate against out-of-staters with regard to fundamental rights or important economic activities. The Clause provides another way in which states are prohibited from discriminating against citizens of other states in favor of their own. We study it right after the Dormant Commerce Clause because both can be used to challenge state and local laws that discriminate against out-of-staters, but the Privileges and Immunities Clause differs from the Dormant Commerce Clause in that it (1) only applies to out-of-staters; and (2) only applies to citizens.

The clearest application of the Privileges and Immunities Clause comes from *United Building & Trades Council v. Mayor and Council of Camden* (1984) (Rehnquist). A Camden, N.J., ordinance required that at least forty percent of employees of contractors and subcontractors working on city construction projects be city residents. The Court set forth a two-step analysis:

1. **Does the ordinance burden one of those privileges and immunities protected by the clause?** The Court answered yes; it interfered with the pursuit of employment, a *fundamental privilege and immunity "bearing upon the vitality of the Nation as a single entity."*[13]

2. **Is there a substantial reason to justify the difference in treatment between in-state and out-of-state residents?** The Court set up a sort of intermediate scrutiny (and remanded for a factual finding as to whether Camden's economic and social ills justified the ordinance).

What's the takeaway? The Privileges and Immunities Clause *limits the ability of one state to discriminate against out-of-staters*

[13] United Bldg. & Const. Trades Council v. Mayor of Camden, 465 U.S. 208, 218 (1984).

with regard to fundamental rights or important economic activities. It provides another way in which states are prohibited from discriminating against citizens of other states in favor of their own. There is a two-step analysis in which these questions must be answered: (1) has the state discriminated against out-of-staters with regard to privileges and immunities that it accords its own citizens? (2) if there is such discrimination, is there a sufficient justification for the discrimination? This creates a strong (but not absolute) presumption against state and local laws that discriminate against out-of-staters with regard to fundamental rights or important economic activities.

Why do we read and discuss the Privileges and Immunities Clause? It ties in with the bigger theme of the relationship between the states and the nation. As the *Camden* Court wrote, the "The Commerce Clause acts as an *implied restraint upon state regulatory powers.* Such powers *must give way* before the superior authority of Congress to legislate on (or leave unregulated) matters involving interstate commerce."[14] This reaffirmation of Dormant Commerce Clause analysis ties in with the Privileges and Immunities Clause, which deals with discrimination against out-of-staters, not interstate commerce per se. But all are connected in the national patchwork economy.

P.S. In case you're wondering, *Supreme Court of New Hampshire v. Piper* (1985) (Powell) holds that Bar admission is a privilege that cannot be restricted to in-state residents.

E. Preemption

Preemption follows on the previous discussions, providing one final limitation on state abilities to regulate, based on the existence of a national government. As we just saw, in the *absence* of

[14] Id. at 220.

congressional action, a state's action may still be unconstitutional, under either Dormant Commerce Clause or Privileges and Immunities analysis. But *if Congress has acted, federal action may **preempt** state action.* Why? Preemption analysis stems from the Supremacy Clause, Article VI, Section 2: "the laws of the United States. . . shall be the Supreme Law of the Land."[15] *If there is a conflict between federal and state or local law, the former preempts the latter.*

Preemption occurs in two major situations.

1. *Express.* Federal law may expressly preempt state or local law.
2. *Implied.* Preemption may be implied by a clear congressional intent to preempt state or local law. Within this category, there's also (a) field preemption; and (b) conflict preemption.

Pacific Gas & Electric v. State Energy Resources Commission (1983) (White) provides a helpful example. The federal government had regulated the field of nuclear power plants and nuclear safety in the Atomic Energy Act ("AEA") and with the Nuclear Regulatory Commission ("NRC"). The state of California then placed a moratorium on nuclear power plant construction until adequate waste disposal methods were available and approved by a federal agency. PG&E argued that the California law was preempted by the federal statute—the argument was that the *state regulation fell within the field that the federal government had preserved for its own* control. Either *expressly* or *impliedly,* the argument went, Congress could keep states from entering this field of regulation. But the Court disagreed and held that Congress did not expressly take over or preempt *all* state action in the field. Congress intended for the federal government to have exclusive authority to regulate

[15] US Const. art. VI, § 2.

safety, but "the states retain their traditional responsibility in the field of regulating electrical utilities for determining questions of need, reliability, cost and other related state concerns."[16] Thus the Court held that the California law was not preempted by the AEA because *its main purpose was economics, not safety*. "[W]e accept California's avowed economic purpose as the rationale for enacting [its act]. Accordingly, the *statute lies outside the occupied field* of nuclear safety regulation."[17]

The Court also rejected PG&E's argument that the California law *conflicted* with federal regulation of nuclear waste disposal, interfering with a federal objective of encouraging the development of nuclear power. Here, the argument was that there was some sort of implied *conflict preemption*. The Court upheld the state law, holding that while the federal AEA and NRC clearly regulated the *handling* of spent fuel, they did not address the *economics* of providing energy to consumers, which was the realm of the California law.

What's the takeaway? There are two major situations in which preemption occurs. First, *federal law may expressly preempt state or local law*. Second, *preemption may be implied by a clear congressional intent to preempt state or local law*. There are two sub-options: (a) **field preemption**: where *the scheme of federal regulation is so pervasive as to make reasonable the inference that Congress left no room for the States to supplement it—the federal law occupies the field*; and (b) **conflict preemption**: where *compliance with both federal and state laws is a physical impossibility, or where state law stands as an obstacle to the accomplishment and execution of the full purposes and objectives of Congress*.

---

[16] Pac. Gas & Elec. Co. v. State Energy Res. Conservation & Dev. Comm'n, 461 U.S. 190, 205 (1983).

[17] Id. at 216 (emphasis added).

Why do we read and discuss preemption? This is another example of the balance of power between the states and the federal government. *PG&E* shows us something about both horizontal and vertical power relationships. On the one hand we see an example of *vertical* relationships—between the nation and states. The Supremacy Clause places nation above state, but it's not absolute. The nation cannot do anything it wants, for the states have many defined powers, and the Tenth Amendment reserves powers to them as well. Also, *PG&E* involves a question of *horizontal* power struggles as well, as the U.S. Supreme Court is defining (limiting) the reach of a federal statute passed by Congress. The Court thus can rein in federal legislative power in a way that implies both.

Also, it is important to see that the key to California's victory was in successfully **framing** the issue. The moratorium law was characterized as an *economic* issue rather than *safety* issue, as the state argued that it was just trying to stop power shortages and electricity price increases. In California in the 1970s, the issue of nuclear safety was front and center. It is hard to imagine that nobody in the state saw this as a way to protect against what they perceived to be dangerous nuclear power plants. But the majority on the U.S. Supreme Court didn't see that, as they ruled that the state statute was *not* preempted by the federal law regulating nuclear safety. In deciding whether California's law was preempted, the Court had to (1) characterize the federal objective; and then (2) characterize the state law and purpose. If the AEA were read broadly, then the state law, which encroached on it, would have been preempted. Instead, the Court avoided finding preemption by more narrowly characterizing the federal goal. Alternatively, if the Court had characterized California's aim as broadly ensuring safety, then its law would have been preempted. The Court avoided finding preemption by accepting California's claim that its goal was economic, even though the law was written in terms of preventing construction of nuclear power plants unless safety of disposal was assured.

Preemption, in a sense, is something we've all learned from childhood. I have an older sister, and sometimes—just sometimes—I would annoy her. It would start with one tiny finger and a poke in the shoulder. Then another, and perhaps one more. She would complain(!), and my parents would say: "Stop touching your sister!!" The explicit rule was not to touch. So, what did I do? I would get as close as possible, with that same finger extended. Right next to her face. When the screaming would start, I would come back, "But you said not to touch her, and I'm not touching her!" For a number of reasons, that argument would lose, but the point is that the rule was really to leave her alone. If it was only about the subset of not touching, then perhaps I could have won my point. But whatever my parents said was the supreme law of the land; and when Congress regulates in an area, that is also the supreme law of the land. In preemption cases, you have to look at the overarching goals of a federal enactment, then the specific statutory language, and lay them side-by-side with the state regulation to see if there's any preemption.

CHAPTER 6

Spending and Taxing Powers

There is a small bit of case law and a little attention in Con Law paid to a few additional areas: the Taxing Power, the Spending Power, the War Power, and the Treaty Power. There is fairly little case law on the Spending and Taxing clauses, so this discussion will be fairly short and happy. Also, you will note that analysis under both clauses is rather similar and overlapping. The most pertinent and interesting issues that you will deal with in terms of foreign affairs powers come in the context of other materials in the next chapter, dealing with Separation of Powers and the War on Terror. So for now, we will make this a quick look at the Spending Clause and Taxing Clause.

In Article I, Section 8, the Constitution grants Congress broad power to spend funds to advance the general welfare. *United States v. Butler* (1936) (Roberts) helped explain these limits, as the Court reviewed the Agricultural Adjustment Act of 1933. The Act sought to stabilize farm prices by curtailing production—in effect it authorized the Secretary of Agriculture to pay farmers not to grow their crops. Funds to pay farmers were made available from collection of a processing tax on commodities. The law was challenged by a cotton processor arguing that it was an unconstitutional congressional attempt to regulate local agriculture. The Court first affirmed its own basic function in our government: "When an act of Congress is appropriately challenged in the courts as not conforming to the constitutional mandate the judicial branch of the Government has only one duty—to lay the article of the Constitution which is invoked beside the statute which is challenged and to decide whether the latter squares with the former. [. . .] This court neither approves nor condemns any legislative policy."[1] In other words, the Court must defer to policy choices of Congress and not be a second-guessing super-legislature making policy decisions, as long as the legislative branch is acting within its powers.

The textual roots in Article I, Section 8 provide for a congressional (taxing and) spending power, but without much definition. The *Butler* Court weighed two competing views:

- **Madison**: the spending power is limited to those powers enumerated in Article I, Section 8.
- **Hamilton**: the clause provides a broader power; the (taxing and) spending power is only limited by the need to provide for the general welfare of the country.

The Court endorsed the Hamiltonian view, reading the spending power broadly. That, however, did not necessarily make this law constitutional. While the Court interpreted Congress' power to tax and spend broadly, it did not endorse an unlimited power, and the specific law in question was held unconstitutional. As a matter of general principle, the Court declared, "The Congress cannot invade state jurisdiction to compel individual action; no

1 United States v. Butler, 297 U.S. 1, 62-63 (1936).

more can it purchase such action."[2] And with regard to this particular measure "Congress has no power to enforce its commands on the farmer to the ends sought by the [Act]. It must follow that it may not indirectly accomplish those ends by taxing and spending to purchase compliance."[3]

What's the takeaway? *Congress is not limited to spending only to achieve the specific powers enumerated in Article I. Congress has leeway to spend in furtherance of the general welfare, as long as it does not violate some other constitutional provision.*

Why do we read and discuss this? We need to put this in the context of the other New Deal era cases. This case was decided in 1936, and can be seen as part of the build-up to Roosevelt's Court-packing plan. The Court had been barring Congress from acting pursuant to its commerce power to regulate intrastate economic activity (see Chapter 4). In *Butler,* the Court held that Congress is barred from using spending conditions to achieve such regulation indirectly through other means, thus reining in Congress. Even while adopting a broader (Hamiltonian) view of the spending power, the Court rejected a New Deal program, exercising its power to protect states and farmers from the reach of the federal government.

One modern interpretation of the Spending Clause came in 1987 in *South Dakota v. Dole* (Rehnquist). In 1984 Congress passed legislation directing the Secretary of Transportation to withhold 5% of federal highway funds from states with drinking ages below 21. In effect, the federal law sought to create a national 21-year-old drinking age by withholding funds from state and local governments that failed to impose such a drinking age. But each state is in charge of its own drinking laws—this is regarded as a proper exercise of the police power at the state level. The federal government argued that this was only a *condition* on the expenditure of funds, permissible

2 Id. at 73.

3 Id. at 74.

under the spending power. South Dakota (which sold low-alcohol beer to 19-year-olds) attacked the law as a thinly veiled attempt to achieve that which the federal government cannot do, under the guise of the congressional spending power.

The Court held this condition on spending to be constitutional, even assuming that Congress could not mandate a national drinking age directly. The Court laid out four criteria for spending power analysis:

1. a purpose to serve the general welfare;
2. a clear statement of the condition;
3. germaneness: relationship between the condition and the purpose of the spending;
4. no inducement to states to violate any independently protected constitutional rights.

The opinion most thoroughly explored the germaneness prong. The Court was deferential, holding that Congress could rationally have thought that teenage drinking leads to drunk driving, which leads to highway accidents, which increases danger and operating costs of highways. Despite the possible lack of congressional power to impose a national drinking age, the Court found the condition on the federal highway money to be only a "relatively mild encouragement"[4] and deemed it constitutional. To the contrary, a dissenting Justice O'Connor said that deeming this law as constitutional was too much of a stretch. Instead, she sought a showing of a substantial relationship between a funding condition and a federal interest reflected in expenditure.

Now looking at *both* tax and spend powers, in *NFIB v. Sebelius* (2012) (Roberts), the Court upheld the individual mandate in the Affordable Care Act as a proper exercise of Taxing Clause powers,

---

[4] South Dakota v. Dole, 483 U.S. 203, 211 (1987).

and rejected it as exceeding the Spending Clause (we looked at the Commerce Clause aspects of the decision in Chapter 4). By a 5-4 vote, the Court sustained the individual mandate as a properly enacted tax. The individual mandate imposes a tax, even though not labeled explicitly as such: "The exaction the Affordable Care Act imposes on those without health insurance looks like a tax in many respects."[5] As the individual mandate is "designed to affect individual conduct [and] raise considerable revenue,"[6] it is comparable to many taxes previously upheld as within the taxing power. The Court held that Congress possesses the power to impose that tax to enforce the individual mandate in the Affordable Care Act. While the Chief Justice wrote that there are limits on the taxing power, he did not spell them out specifically. (Perhaps the spending power analysis can help.)

While upholding the individual mandate as within the taxing power, the Court held that it exceeded the spending power. Applying *South Dakota v. Dole*, the Court considered whether Congress crossed the line from that case, and also the coercion line established in cases like *New York v. U.S.* (also discussed in Chapter 4). Chief Justice Roberts wrote that "the financial 'inducement' Congress has chosen is much more than 'relatively mild encouragement'—it is a gun to the head."[7] Under that analysis, the Court held that Congress went too far.

What's the takeaway on spending and taxing power analysis? Congress possesses an expansive power to spend for the general welfare so long as it does not violate another constitutional provision. Congress may *impose conditions* on grants to state and local governments so long as the conditions relate (are germane) to the purpose of the spending and are clearly stated. (And for short

---

5 NFIB v. Sebelius, 567 U.S. 519, 563 (2012).

6 Id. at 567.

7 Id. at 581.

and happy purposes, also note that you have a four-part test to apply!) Similarly, the taxing power appears broad, but not unlimited, with the boundaries still to be clarified by the Court.

Why do we read and discuss these cases? The interesting issue here is where to draw lines. The Court reached different outcomes in *South Dakota v. Dole* and *NFIB v. Sebelius*, comparing the 5% denial of transportation funds in the former, with the possible complete denial of Medicaid funds in the latter. The question then becomes, *where is the tipping point between 5% and 100%?* And in answering that, connect these case with the current, more restrictive view of the congressional commerce power and more expansive view of Tenth Amendment protections of the States. In the post-*Lopez* era (see Chapter 4), could Congress condition a grant of funds to increase school safety on a state enactment of a law criminalizing gun possession in a school zone? Would that be germane to the expenditure? What if Congress conditions a grant of general education funds on enactment of such a law? Would that impermissibly regulate in the realm that *Lopez* said (in dictum) is reserved for state control? After *Printz*, would requiring state officials to perform Brady checks be unconstitutional if made a condition of state receipt of law enforcement funds? Applying *South Dakota v. Dole*, if conditions are insufficiently germane to the funding purposes, they are improperly coercive, but if not, we still might run up against the commandeering issues from *U.S. v. New York* and *Printz*, as the Court held in *NFIB v. Sebelius*.

CHAPTER 7

Separation of Powers

A. Limits on Executive Power in Foreign Affairs

Why did the Framers decide to separate governmental powers? Though that decision created an inefficient system, our branched system of government prevents the concentration of power, maintains checks and balances, and is decentralized to ensure liberty. While we loosely throw around the term separation of powers, the branches' individual governmental functions are not so distinctly separate. There is considerable overlap, for example, in the legislative process, as Congress passes and presents legislation, but the President may veto; in foreign affairs, the President negotiates treaties and appoints ambassadors, but Congress ratifies and confirms them; the President is the Commander-in-Chief of the armed forces, but Congress is delegated the power to declare war and raise armies and navies. That's all to say that our system thrives on checks and balances that come from both the blending and the separating of powers. Accordingly, an important challenge our courts face is the responsibility of figuring out when any one branch is improperly encroaching on the sphere of another.

The seminal case you will read in this area is *Youngstown Sheet & Tube Co. v. Sawyer* (1952) (Black) (also known as *The Steel Seizure Case*). The case arose during the Korean War and raised the question of whether the President has inherent powers beyond those specified in Constitution. In short, there was a labor dispute between steel companies and employees, and various efforts to settle the dispute failed. On April 4, 1952, the United Steelworkers announced a planned nationwide strike. In response, President Truman issued an Executive Order directing Commerce Secretary Charles Sawyer to take possession of the steel mills and keep them running. Truman did so because he believed that a steel strike could endanger the national defense and the war effort in Korea. This was not an exercise of an explicit power granted to the President in Article II of the Constitution. Truman tried to justify this as an emergency executive action emerging from his position as Commander-in-Chief in charge of military efforts. But Congress hadn't given the president the power to act on this issue, even though they could have, so he wasn't executing any specific law.

There were seven separate opinions, with Justice Black writing for the majority. He basically argued that there are *no inherent presidential powers*: the President's actions must be confined to what the Constitution or Congress explicitly allows him to do. Justice Black made a formal distinction between legislative and executive power, arguing that the President may act only pursuant to express or clearly implied statutory or constitutional authority. "The President's power, if any, to issue the order must stem either from an act of Congress or from the Constitution itself. There is no statute that expressly authorizes the President to take possession of property as he did here, [and] it is not claimed that express constitutional language grants this power to the President."[1] *There is no inherent presidential power; the President may act only if*

---

1 Youngstown Sheet & Tube Co. v. Sawyer, 343 U.S. 579, 585, 587 (1952).

there is express constitutional or statutory authority. So the Court held that the seizure order was an unconstitutional legislative act without prior constitutional or congressional authorization.

Justice Frankfurter concurred, but he took a more functional and flexible approach than Justice Black, seeing some significance in Congress' failure to speak. His view was that, theoretically, the President is allowed to take any action that is not constitutionally or statutorily prohibited. But, in this situation, Congress had decided not to grant the President authority to seize the steel mills, a clear decision to preclude such presidential action. By doing so, "Congress has expressed its will to withhold this power from the President as though it had said so in so many words."[2] Such rejection implicitly negated executive authority.

The concurrence by Justice Jackson in large part agreed with Justice Frankfurter's, in that it viewed Truman's action as incompatible with congressional will. But more than that, his opinion (despite it not coming with a majority) has become the primary test for how to weigh executive powers. He wrote that there is a three-part division of presidential power:

1. Executive power is at its "maximum" when, in addition to Article II power, the President can rely on express or implied authority from Congress. "When the President acts pursuant to an express or implied authorization of Congress, his authority is at its maximum, for it includes all that he possesses in his own right plus all that Congress can delegate."[3] Under such circumstances, the President's acts are presumptively valid.

[2] Id. at 602 (Frankfurter, J., concurring).

[3] Id. at 635 (Jackson, J., concurring).

2. "When the President acts in absence of either a congressional grant or denial of authority, he can rely only upon his own independent powers, but there is a *zone of twilight* in which he and Congress may have concurrent authority, or in which the distribution of authority is uncertain."[4] In this ill-defined twilight zone, the President's power must come from Article II alone.

3. "When the President takes measures incompatible with the expressed or implied will of Congress, his power is at its lowest ebb."[5] Because the President in such a situation would be disobeying federal law, such presidential actions would be allowed only if the law enacted by Congress is unconstitutional.

In this situation, Jackson concluded that though the President has inherent powers as Commander-in-Chief (Art. II, Sec. 2, cl. 1), Congress has the primary responsibility to raise and support an Army, and provide and maintain a Navy (Art. I, Sec. 8, cl. 12 and 13). This situation fell under that power. The President "has no monopoly of 'war powers,' whatever they are."[6] To rule otherwise would signal no foreseeable limit to presidential power, on the way to dictatorship.

What's the takeaway? Despite seven different opinions, there's *one* to focus on: Justice Jackson's three-part framework for how to analyze when the President has acted in the shadowy areas between executive and legislative power. Every analysis has to explore those three levels of presidential power: (1) *maximum authority* when both the Constitution and Congress grant power; (2) a *twilight zone*, when there is no congressional authorization; and

---

4 Id. at 637 (emphasis added).

5 Id. at 637.

6 Id. at 644.

(3) the *lowest ebb* when the President acts contrary to the express will of Congress.

Why do we read and discuss this material? The *Steel Seizure Case* helps us unpack the broader issues of separation of powers. The Court specifically acknowledges the textual foundation that divides the powers but then helps sort the key question of what lies between. In so doing, the Court not only declares the powers of each branch, but also asserts its own power as the arbiter of these matters. Each branch has a role to play, and the Court's, at times, may be the *most* powerful. As winds of popular sentiment blow, moving the political branches, constitutional rights are often challenged, and in such circumstances the courts stand up for the rule of law and constitutionalism.

In *Zivotofsky v. Kerry* (2015) (Kennedy), the Court applied Justice Jackson's three-part analytical framework from *The Steel Seizure Case* to a question involving the president's recognition power in foreign affairs. The question arose in the very specific context of whether the U.S. government would list "Jerusalem" or "Jerusalem, Israel" on the passport of an American citizen born there. Congress had written a law which, in effect, commanded the Secretary of State to indicate "Jerusalem, Israel" on a passport, if the holder requested, in contrast to the President's policy that would state the place of birth as "Jerusalem." (The broader context ran back to 1948 when President Truman formally recognized Israel, and ran through the decades across all presidents and congresses.)

Justice Kennedy saw this as a situation in the third category of *The Steel Seizure* framework, as Congress had explicitly legislated one way and the President sought to act in the opposite direction. In such a situation, the Court's analysis focused on what powers the Constitution granted to the president alone. The Court explored the text and structure of the Constitution, case law, the Federalist Papers, and historical practice, and found a clear rule that "the formal determination of recognition is a power to be exercised only by the President."[7] The Court further examined the law in conflict and wrote: "The Executive's exclusive power extends no further than his formal recognition determination. But as to that determination, Congress may not enact a law that directly contradicts it."[8] The Court observed the importance of the nation speaking with one voice in such maters—the president's—and thus struck the law as unconstitutional.

Note also, while not applying *Youngstown*, the Court looked at the question of executive power in a high-profile case recently, *Trump v. Hawaii* (2018) (Roberts).[9] In this case, the Court upheld the Executive Order which suspended the entry of certain individuals from specified nations into the United States (known as the *Travel Ban* or the *Muslim Ban*, depending on who you ask). The key point for our purposes here (not addressing the Establishment Clause issues which are outside the scope of this book) is that the Court found that the directly relevant statute, the Immigration and Nationality Act, "exudes deference to the President in every clause."[10] The Court upheld the Executive Order, enforcing that deference.

The *Steel Seizure* framework controls analysis of the question "What inherent powers does the President possess?" The President has explicit powers, but do any implicit powers exist in terms of war or emergency, particularly in light of congressional activity or inactivity? The issue has been front and center in our country and across the globe ever since 9/11, as we have seen a wide range of executive decisions in response to the 9/11 attacks and subsequent military action. Contrary to much of what you will read in Con Law, these next cases are (as they say in *Law & Order*) "ripped from the

[7] Zivotofsky v. Kerry 576 U.S. 1, 23 (2015).

[8] Id. at 30.

[9] Trump v. Hawaii, 585 U.S. 667 (2018).

[10] Id. at 684.

headlines." While there are many cases, we will explore three in greater depth, which show how the Court can assert itself to balance powers and protect individual rights simultaneously.

Before we get to these cases, let me also touch on some older case law first (can't avoid the old stuff completely, can we?), as there is some key historical precedent. First, there's the writ of *habeas corpus*, also known as the Great Writ. It is a common law right to challenge the power of the King (or, in America, the executive) to detain an individual. It requires the jailer to demonstrate sufficient legal justification to hold the individual in jail. So if an individual is unlawfully detained, the Great Writ ensures that the prisoner should be released. The remedy can be sought by the prisoner or by another person on the prisoner's behalf. It has ancient roots in England and is considered to be a central legal tool to secure individual liberty against the excesses of the state. In the United States, the right is protected by the Suspension Clause of the Constitution (Art. I, Sec. 9, cl. 2), which requires the existence of the writ unless suspended by Congress, but only in case of "Rebellion or Invasion."

So, that's the textual foundation, and *Ex Parte Milligan* (1866) (Davis) sheds some light on the issue. During the Civil War President Lincoln attempted to try a civilian in a military tribunal, but he was rebuked by the Court. The Justices held that for civilians, only civilian courts are the proper venue for trial, not military tribunals. *Ex Parte Quirin* (1942) (Stone) was a World War II case, which emphasized the importance of a couple of basic rules regarding the laws of war: (1) uniformed soldiers are lawful combatants, immune from prosecution for killing other soldiers and entitled to humane treatment if captured; and (2) unlawful combatants are civilians (not members of armed forces) who engage in hostilities. Unlike lawful combatants, unlawful ones can be tried and punished for those acts. Beyond these specifics, it is important to see the broader view that over two centuries, a set of rules was established, with laws of war in which nations were pitted against each other, and soldiers who wore uniforms and engaged each other on battlefields. When captured on the battlefield, those soldiers were entitled to certain basic treatment, rights, and privileges, ultimately including release after the cessation of hostilities, i.e., surrender and/or a peace treaty.

That was then. And this is now, in a post-9/11 world where countless "enemy combatants" have been apprehended as part of the global war on terror post-9/11. Guantanamo Bay has served as the detention site for unknown hundreds or thousands of such individuals. While Guantanamo is, geographically speaking, part of Cuba, it is under complete American control. The *Hamdi v. Rumsfeld* (2004) (O'Connor) case involved an American citizen who was captured on the battlefield in Afghanistan. His father sought a *habeas* petition on his behalf. The Bush Administration argued that Hamdi was caught on the battlefield in armed conflict against the United States, so he was an "enemy combatant."

Therefore, the question became who could be deemed an enemy combatant in the new age of the war on terror, and who could make such a determination. Statutorily, the Authorization of the Use of Military Force, passed by Congress after 9/11, justified detention, in addition to the general principles of the laws of war. At its core, the question was about the limits of presidential power, specifically, the limits of the power to detain and interrogate individuals deemed to be enemy combatants. "The threshold question before us is whether the Executive has the authority to detain citizens who qualify as 'enemy combatants.' "[11] The Court's answer: "We [. . .] hold that a citizen-detainee seeking to challenge his classification as an enemy combatant must receive notice of the factual basis for his classification and a fair opportunity to rebut the

---

[11] Hamdi v. Rumsfeld, 542 U.S. 507, 516 (2004).

Government's factual assertions before a neutral decision maker. [. . .] These essential constitutional promises must not be eroded."[12] The courts have a central role. The basic protections of *habeas* apply. The Court still made clear, however, that the exigencies of the circumstances may demand that the government be given flexibility to deny some individual rights in terms of procedure. The central premise supporting the opinion is to reject "a heavily circumscribed role for the courts. . . We have long since made clear that a state of war is not a blank check for the President when it comes to the rights of the Nation's citizens."[13] Specifically in this context, the Great Writ is the judiciary's check on the Executive, unless Congress suspends it through proper constitutional means. Thus, the Court addressed the key questions of what process is due to individuals in this situation.

What's the takeaway from *Hamdi*? The Constitution still grounds us, even in the post-9/11 world, and *Americans have* habeas *rights, no matter where they are captured, or where they are imprisoned. War is not a blank check to excuse those basic due process requirements.*

The Court waded deeper into this area two years later in *Hamdan v. Rumsfeld* (2006) (Stevens), which reinforced that despite attempts through two significant pieces of legislation, Congress cannot give the military or the Executive branch the authority to convene military commissions and suspend people's *habeas* rights. Most importantly, the Court held that at a minimum, Common Article 3 of the Geneva Convention applies to the conflict with al Qaeda. Common Article 3 prohibits torture and any "inhumane" treatment. Thus, even for al Qaeda prisoners in American-controlled detention sites all over world, torture is not permissible.

---

[12] Id. at 533.

[13] Id. at 535-536.

Boumediene v. Bush (2008) (Kennedy) gave us one last look at the current state of affairs. The Military Commission Act of 2006 ("MCA") was intended to effectively repeal the *habeas* statute as applied to Guantanamo, reversing another related decision in this series, *Rasul v. Bush* (2004) (Stevens). The MCA substituted alternative review procedures. In *Rasul*, the Court affirmed the central role of *habeas* in a constitutional system as a check on arbitrary executive power. And it further affirmed that the Court itself protects the same *habeas* rights that have always existed.

Additionally and importantly, in Boumediene, while the government argued that Guantanamo was not subject to such oversight since it was on foreign soil, the Court held that its reach is determined not by formal sovereignty, but instead on the level of actual, *de facto* control over territory. If the U.S. government exercises substantial control, which it certainly does in Guantanamo, and no obstacles would prevent the extension of U.S. law, then the writ should stand. The Court rejected what it saw as the government's attempt to evade legal constraint on non-U.S. soil. Given that the U.S. government exercises total control and jurisdiction over Guantanamo, and that there are no practical obstacles to extending the writ, the Court held that basic procedural protections must apply; *if* habeas *is not available, then the government must replace it with an "adequate substitute."*[14] A review of the Guantanamo proceedings revealed them to be constitutionally inadequate: it was not an adversarial system; it did not allow sufficient evidence to be presented or challenged; overall it was a closed system. The Court contrasted *habeas* as a remedy that cannot be so constrained, with the Court instructing that the writ requires that the accused be given an opportunity to prove factual innocence.

---

[14] Boumediene v. Bush, 553 U.S. 723, 779 (2008).

What's the takeaway? Even though Congress had statutorily authorized military commissions, *the MCA failed to provide an adequate substitute for the* habeas *rights it denied aliens.* Even though we are dealing here with a non-American citizen, these basic procedural rights extend to individuals wherever the U.S. government exercises control, so the MCA was found unconstitutional. This is a very robust exercise of judicial power. (In June 2012 the Supreme Court denied review of one more Guantanamo case, *Abdah v. Obama*, further cementing the conventional wisdom that the high court will not be adding anything more to its current body of case law in the area.)

Why do we read and discuss these cases? At the core, it's about the *textual division of power*: Congress declares war, and the President is Commander-in-Chief. But the trick is that the cases explore the question of what powers and what authority lie in between the lines of the Constitution; what inherent executive authority exists? *Youngstown* is a classic case of separation of powers. But we take another step and the Court reveals even more when we get into the Guantanamo cases. The Court enters the fray very forcefully, so the separation of powers question is about *all three branches*. Over a series of cases, the Court gives Congress a slap on the wrist, then Congress tries to respond to the Court while still retaining its goal, only for the Court to slap its wrist again, perhaps even harder. **The Court declares that it has a role to play in this important point in American history. It actively steps into that role, and defines the substance and scope of that role. In doing so, the Court ultimately protects individual rights; these cases re-state and reinforce due process rights for individuals being held by the American government. The Court stands up for the individual against the excesses of the state, balancing security and liberty. The Court stands up for the Constitution against the actions of the political branches.**

Another interesting reason why we read and discuss these recent cases is that they are important and influential current events. So it is worth having current events knowledge and perspective. Today, wars are fought completely differently from how they were in the past. The old case law deals with wars declared by nations, fought on battlefields, with soldiers in uniform. The Court struggled to ensure the security of the nation as the Congress and President carried out their roles. But in the context of the "war on terror" with the compounding factors of enemies who aren't always clearly known or identified, a potentially never-ending time frame, and a unique situation in Guantanamo, wars today are fought differently. It is a lesson about **the concept of Emergency Constitutionalism (or perhaps the lack thereof).** The Court instructs that even today with a new, dangerous enemy or threat in our midst, **no specific additional powers exist in times of emergency, without some check from the Judicial Branch interpreting the Constitution.**

B. Limits on Executive Power in Domestic Affairs

The previous cases presented the separation of powers analysis on the international front, and now we look at the domestic side. Still, the starting point is where one branch's powers begin and another's end, with the Court as the arbiter. Two cases help us as we move forward. First, *INS v. Chadha* (1983) (Burger) involved a student from India whose visa had expired. A U.S. immigration judge (working for the executive branch) ordered that he could stay in the country. It was basically an administrative procedure halting his deportation. In effect, Congress wrote and passed a bill that was signed into law; the law then was executed, so it would seem that would end the story—Chadha would stay in the country. But the

House of Representatives adopted a resolution overturning the executive decision, thereby ordering Chadha's deportation.

Under what authority did the House act? The federal law gave either house of Congress the authority to overturn the executive branch decision to suspend deportation. Legislatively this was not uncommon; many statutes contained *legislative veto* provisions, intended to check unaccountable executive actions. It was a legislative innovation that reflected considerable political maneuvering from the Executive and Legislative branches, seeking efficiency and power-sharing. But that was problematic. "The fact that a given law or procedure is efficient, convenient, and useful in facilitating functions of government, standing alone, will not save it if it is contrary to the Constitution."[15] This was held to be an unconstitutional legislative veto. *Why?* Congress may only legislate if there is *bicameralism*—passage by both the House and Senate—and *presentment*—giving the bill to the President to sign or veto. *What is the textual foundation?* Article I, Section 7, cl. 2. The legislative veto was held to be legislation without either the necessary bicameralism or presentment. Therefore, *the legislative veto is unconstitutional.*

The key principle here was that the separation of powers is necessary to ensure a workable government without excessive concentration of power, or the arbitrary exercise of power. The majority's approach can be described as *formalist*, looking somewhat narrowly at the form of the constitutional structure, asking four questions:

1. *Are powers separable?* Yes, the powers can be categorically distinguished;
2. *What is the harm in the absence of separation?* The harm to be avoided is the commingling of powers—

[15] I.N.S. v. Chadha, 462 U.S. 919, 944 (1983).

the government must function in a way that lets the individual know how and where to resolve matters and seek help;

3. *Analytical approach?* The best way to avoid the improper commingling of powers is to adhere as literally as possible to the constitutional text and its division of powers amongst the branches;

4. *What judicial deference is due?* Active judicial intervention is required because political safeguards are insufficient to stop self-aggrandizing political branches.

As another example, let's look at *Clinton v. New York* (1998) (Stevens), which is sort of the flip-side of *Chadha*, involving the Line Item Veto Act. In a sense, it was simple: Congress passed a bill (the Line Item Veto Act) to give the President more power; the President signed it; the Act gave such power (willingly) to the President, and he then exercised that power—*so what was the problem?* The law attempted to give the President a line-item veto, i.e., the power to "cancel in whole," that is, reject, three types of provisions that could be signed into law: (1) specific dollar amounts of discretionary spending; (2) new spending items; (3) any limited tax benefit. President Clinton exercised this power to cancel some Medicaid funding for New York and a tax provision to benefit certain food processors. Constitutionally speaking, however, the President amended two acts of Congress, after passage, by repealing portions. Look at Article I, Section 7: "Every bill which shall have passed the House of Representatives and the Senate, shall, before it become a law, be presented to the President of the United States; If he approve he shall sign it, but if not he shall return it, with his objections."[16] The President must sign it or veto it. All of it. The

[16] U.S. Const. art. I § 7.

Constitution does not allow for the actions permitted and carried out through the Line Item Veto Act. *This was a violation of constitutional principle—the President was acting outside the executive sphere.* The Constitution provides for a *constitutional return* of the *entire* bill, before it becomes law. But the Act provided for a *statutory cancellation* of *part* of the bill after it had become law. While the line-item veto is popular in many governments, with the vast majority of States still having some form of line-item veto power pursuant to their own constitutions, this was not a policy matter. Rather, this was a constitutional question and the only proper way to bring about change would be through amendment. So this is similar to *Chadha,* resting on the formal structures by which laws are enacted.

What's the takeaway? *In order to properly execute the legislative process, there must be* ***bicameralism****, passage by both houses of Congress, and* ***presentment****, giving the bill to the President for signature or veto. Anything less is unconstitutional.*

Why do we read and discuss these cases? *They give us concrete readings about separation of powers and raise broad ideas of what may be called formalism v. functionalism.* As noted above, in each case the majority reads the text in a more formalist way—you must follow (as nearly as possible) the exact form of the Constitution in matters of separation of powers. Instead of the majority's more narrow view, the dissent in these cases encouraged what might be called a *functionalist* view, encouraging innovation. This suggests a more flexible and evolutionary approach, rather than original or literalist. The core idea is to *follow the Constitution in substance, even if not in detailed form.* As a result, that interpretation allows the Court to defer more to the political branches, who (being natural rivals) can be trusted to look after their own interests and to check each other's overreach. This debate is broadly important as an analytical tool for basic constitutional interpretation, tying in with debates between originalism (or perhaps strict construction), and more evolutionary Constitution expounding.

Here's one last way to think about this, an animated little musical number! In fact, I hope you're already humming to yourself. The song is "I'm Just a Bill" from Schoolhouse Rock. You remember it, I know. Catchy little tune. The video starts with a little boy climbing up the Capitol steps, coming upon a smiley piece of paper. The tired boy says, "You sure gotta climb a lot of steps to get to this Capitol Building here in Washington. But I wonder who that sad little scrap of paper is?"

Cue the music. You know the tune, and here's the song:

I'm just a bill.
Yes, I'm only a bill.
And I'm sitting here on Capitol Hill.
Well, it's a long, long journey
To the capital city.
It's a long, long wait
While I'm sitting in committee,
But I know I'll be a law someday.
At least I hope and pray that I will,
But today I am still just a bill.

With snappy lyrics and a happy little beat, Bill and the boy have a discussion about (yes, you guessed it!) *bicameralism and presentment*, with an easy appeal to the Schoolhouse Rock grade-school audience (and to you, too!). Bill tells of his long journey from an idea, to a bill, moving to committee, to floor debate, to a vote in the House of Representatives. The boy asks, "If they vote yes, what happens?" Bill responds, "Then I go to the Senate and the whole thing starts all over again." Stop humming for a moment. That's bicameralism, right?

If the House votes yes, and the Senate votes yes, then what? Take it to the chorus:

I'm just a bill,
Yes, I'm only a bill.
And if they vote for me on Capitol Hill,
Well, then I'm off to the White House
Where I'll wait in a line
With a lot of other bills
For the president to sign.
And if he signs me, then I'll be a law.
How I hope and pray that he will,
But today I am still just a bill.

The boy interjects, "You mean even if the whole Congress says you should be a law, the president can still say no?" Bill replies, "Yes, that's called a veto. If the President vetoes me, I have to go back to Congress and they vote on me again, and by that time you're so old. . ." The boy cuts in, "By that time it's very unlikely that you'll become a law. It's not easy to become a law, is it?" That's the lesson from *Clinton v. NY*. It's about presentment!

That little song and video tells us just what we learned in those cases. And to bring it to a close (I don't want to leave you hanging), you may be wondering *What happens in the end*? As Bill starts singing again, a Member of Congress rushes up and says, "He signed you, Bill! Now you're a law!" I love a happy ending.

To switch gears to presidential appointments, two recent cases provide additional insights into the nature and meaning of the executive power: *NLRB v. Noel Canning* (2014) (Breyer)[17] and *Lucia v. SEC* (2018) (Kagan).[18]

[17] 573 U.S. 513 (2014).

[18] 585 U.S. 237 (2018).

The Constitution requires the president to obtain the advice and consent of the Senate, in the appointment of certain senior government officials and federal judges. But the Recess Appointments Clause (Art. II, Sec. 2, cl. 3) allows the president to act without such advice and consent, to "[f]ill . . . Vacancies that may happen during the Recess of the Senate, by granting Commissions which shall expire at the End of their next Session."[19] The recess appointment traces back to a time when the Senate could meet with less frequency, as travel was completely different and exponentially more difficult than today, and the Framers had to consider what the president would do if the senators were away from the capital, and urgent needs arose, requiring appointments. *NLRB v. Noel Canning* arose in the context of appointments President Obama made to the National Labor Relations Board and the Consumer Financial Protection Bureau. The Court held that the Recess Appointments Clause authorizes the President to fill any existing vacancy during any recess of sufficient length. However, for purposes of the clause, the Senate is in session (and not in recess) whenever it indicates that it is, as long as (under its own rules), it retains the ability to transact Senate business. While this ruling amounted to a restriction on presidential power, Justice Scalia's concurrence argued that the majority didn't go far enough in limiting the recess appointment power, instead arguing that it should effectively be excised from the Constitution as an anachronism.

In *Lucia v. SEC*, the Court ruled that Administrative Law Judges (ALJs) are considered "Officers of the United States" as defined in the Constitution (Art. II, Sec.2, cl. 2), and they therefore must be appointed by the President or a delegated officer, not simply hired. Like many other government agencies, the Securities and Exchange Commission (SEC) uses ALJs to resolve disputes under its jurisdiction, and they had been hired through an in-house hiring

---

[19] U.S. Const. art. II § 2, cl. 3.

process. Facing an adverse ruling by an ALJ, the petitioner attacked the entire proceeding as invalid, arguing that the ALJ had not been constitutionally appointed to the position. The Court applied its 1991 *Freytag* decision, holding that appointment of SEC ALJs violated the Constitution's appointments clause, because they were appointed by commission staff rather than the commission itself. Because the ALJs possess, in effect, a judicial power under *Freytag*, the Court concluded that SEC ALJs are inferior Officers under the Constitution, and they thus must be appointed by the President or a delegated officer. As the opinion is drafted, it may have far-reaching implications, perhaps as far as extending to invalidate many or even all other ALJ appointments. Recently, in *SEC v. Jarksey* (2024) (Roberts), the Court held that the SEC's use of ALJs in civil penalty cases violated Article I's non-delegation doctrine, by allowing executive employees to exercise the power of Article III judges.

NLRB v. Noel Canning and *Lucia v. SEC* address different but related issues, each with their own specific takeaways. The broader picture as to **why we read and discuss these cases**, is that even with differing perspectives on exactly why, the Justices largely agree on limits on the unilateral reach of the modern executive power.

C. Executive Privilege

The last cases in the separation of powers materials deal with Executive Privilege; the issue of whether the President has some special status by nature of the office he occupies. We start with a story you surely have heard about—Watergate and President Richard Nixon. In the summer of 1972, there was a break-in at the Democratic National Committee headquarters in the Watergate building in Washington, D.C., that set off a chain of events leading to high level White House officials, including Nixon, being linked to a cover-up. Senate hearings on the subject disclosed a secret taping system in the Oval Office, and amid political pressure for an independent investigation, a special prosecutor was appointed. Over the next months, a national drama unfolded over the tapes that Nixon had made, who would get them, and more. This was both a political and a legal storm. As the political pressure mounted, in the spring of 1974, impeachment proceedings started in the House of Representatives pursuant to Article I, Section 2, clause 5. On March 1, a federal grand jury indicted seven top Nixon officials, and named Nixon himself as an unindicted co-conspirator. In April, a subpoena was issued for Nixon to turn over the tapes and other materials to use as possible evidence in an upcoming criminal trial for those accused in the break-in. Nixon refused to comply and moved to quash the subpoena; that motion was denied, and then reviewed by the U.S. Supreme Court, in *United States v. Nixon* (1974) (Burger).

What was Nixon's legal argument behind his refusal to comply? He argued that there is an *absolute Executive Privilege*, a virtual shield to prevent having to turn over these tapes. He argued that principles of separation of powers preclude judicial review. The Court responded with a reaffirmation of the principle that it is the Court's duty to declare the law (remember *Marbury*?). Specifically, as to the privilege question, the Court held that *there is an Executive Privilege, but it is not absolute*. The unanimous opinion stated that the Executive Privilege was not grounded specifically in the text, but instead on a general need for candor in communications with top presidential advisors. However, the privilege must yield to important countervailing interests; an absolute privilege would interfere with the individuals' rights as defendants and with the judiciary's performance of its role to provide fair trials governed by constitutional standards. "[T]he allowance of the privilege to withhold evidence that is demonstrably relevant in a criminal trial would cut deeply into the guarantee of due process of law and gravely impair the basic function of the courts."[20] The need for evidence at the upcoming criminal trial over the break-ins outweighed the constitutional claim of Executive Privilege.

What's the takeaway? U.S. v. Nixon *recognizes the existence of an Executive Privilege, but refuses to make it absolute. It also provides a forceful reaffirmation of the power of Judicial Review and the principle that no person, not even the President, is above the law.*

Yet another presidential scandal came to the Court's attention just over twenty years later in *Clinton v. Jones* (1997) (Stevens). In this situation, President Clinton was sued for allegedly harassing acts directed toward Paula Jones in a hotel when he was governor of Arkansas. While the suit alleged improper actions when he was governor, it was brought while Clinton was the sitting president. Clinton asked for a temporary stay of the suit, arguing that he should not and could not be forced to defend a lawsuit while sitting as President. The Court rejected Clinton's argument for several reasons. First, in another case, *Nixon v. Fitzgerald* (1982) (Powell), the Court had established that there is absolute immunity for acts committed *while in office*, but no such immunity for unofficial conduct. The Court made clear that *Fitzgerald* applied so as to cover only official conduct for acts committed by the individual while sitting as President. There was no extension of the immunity principle to civil litigation involving the President's unofficial conduct outside the scope of the office. Ultimately the Court held that this was a matter of *separation of powers*. The President is not above the law. Article II created the office, and the powers are vested in the individual, so the judicial branch must not impede upon the proper functioning of that individual in that office. At the same time, while the Court agreed with Clinton to an extent and

[20] United States v. Nixon, 418 U.S. 683, 712 (1974).

understood the demands on the individual, they made clear that it does not follow that subjecting the President to judicial proceedings improperly impedes upon Article II functions. Remember, after all, in *U.S. v. Nixon*, the President was subject to judicial process, which significantly burdened his time and life. And in *Clinton v. Jones*, the Justices expressed a belief that this judicial matter would be manageable: "it appears to us highly unlikely to occupy any substantial amount of [President Clinton's] time."[21] Of course, this led to the investigation by Kenneth Starr, revelations about Monica Lewinsky, and impeachment proceedings; but those facts do not resolve the underlying claim about the president being amenable to judicial process.

In *Trump v. United States* (2024) (Roberts) the Court revisited the doctrine of presidential immunity, holding that (1) a president's official acts are presumptively immune from criminal prosecution, and (2) the President's actions which are within his "conclusive and preclusive constitutional authority"[22] are absolutely immune. Following the 2020 election, and the efforts to overturn the results of that election, a federal grand jury indicted (then-former) President Trump,[23] who challenged his indictment. Trump argued that his actions were within "the core of his official duties," and thus deserved absolute immunity.[24] Relying on *Youngstown*, *Fitzgerald*, *Nixon*, and *Jones*, the Court concluded that the separation of powers doctrine and the constitution require presumptive immunity from criminal prosecution for acts "within the outer perimeter of [the President's] official responsibility." While immunity does not exist for unofficial acts, the Court offered guidance for differentiating between official and unofficial acts. One important consideration is the President's authority to take

---

[21] Clinton v. Jones, 520 U.S. 681, 702 (1997).

[22] Trump v. United States, 603 U.S. 593, 607 (2024).

[23] Id. at 609.

[24] Id. at 604.

action, which can be broad. For example, while not derived from statute or the constitution, the President's communications with the American people can be an official act. Further, the Court instructed that courts may not look at the President's motives and an action may be official, although it "allegedly violates a generally applicable law." Applying these principles to the indictment against President Trump, the Court concluded that he had immunity for conversations with Justice Department officials and remanded to the district court for further consideration.[25]

What's the takeaway? *Nixon* reaffirmed the power of the Court to issue subpoenas, as has been the case throughout the nation's history. Likewise the *Clinton* Court held: *"the separation-of-powers doctrine does not require federal courts to stay all private actions against the President until he leaves office."*[26] Presidential immunity extends to official acts committed while in office, but not beyond those bounds. After the *Trump* decision, Presidential power entitles a former President to absolute immunity from criminal prosecution for actions within his conclusive and preclusive constitutional authority, as well as at least presumptive immunity from prosecution for all his official acts. There remains no immunity for unofficial acts.

Why do we read and discuss these cases? They call into question and deliberate a basic principle that used to be clear: *no individual, not even the President of the United States, is above the law.* While there is an Executive Privilege, and while there is broad immunity for actions committed by the President, and while the courts should respect the office in the administration of the judicial system, still, the President may be subject to some judicial process. After the *Trump* decision, the range of executive immunity seems to be quite wide.

---

[25] Following the 2024 election, this case was dismissed.

[26] Clinton v. Jones, 520 U.S. 681, 682 (1997).

It also is important to read these cases because they raise an issue of *impeachment*, which then brings up a number of ideas that run throughout Con Law. Most people agreed that Richard Nixon's acts served as a clear example of impeachable offenses; he was deeply involved in a criminal act designed to influence the presidential election, and the subsequent cover-up in a wide-ranging conspiracy at the highest levels of government. With President Clinton, the charges that were brought by the House involved allegations of lying under oath during an inquiry stemming from a sexual harassment lawsuit. Decades later came the Trump impeachments, the first of which involved allegations of corruption and interference in the 2020 presidential election, specifically Pres. Trump's efforts to solicit Ukraine to become involved in the election. The second impeachment grew from his activities and role in the January 6 Insurrection. So that raises the question: *What is an impeachable offense?* The Constitution provides only the following as a guideline: (Art. II, Sec. 4) "Treason, Bribery, or other High Crimes and Misdemeanors." Is the definition whatever the House (and Senate) says at the time? Possibly. Using the *Baker v. Carr* factors discussed earlier (Chapter 3, Part C), there is a good argument that those are nonjusticiable political questions. Since the Senate did not vote to remove either Clinton or Trump from office and since Nixon was pardoned by his successor Gerald Ford, many questions still remain.

CHAPTER 8

Fundamental Rights and Incorporation

The next four chapters of the book move out of the structural side of Constitutional Law, and into individual rights. That mainly will involve Chapters 9 and 11 on Due Process and Equal Protection. It involves a bigger picture analysis of the Bill of Rights and the post-Civil War Amendments, all of which have transformed the Constitution from a document delineating governmental structures into one which also explicitly speaks to and protects the *individual rights and civil liberties* of its people. As a transition before we look at those specific questions, we discuss Incorporation briefly. While the Constitution expressly protects the nation's citizens from certain actions by the federal government, state and local governments have not always been bound by key provisions of the U.S. Constitution, most notably the Amendments. The following discussion looks at why, as well as how, we ensure that U.S. citizens enjoy the same individual constitutional rights as state citizens, and that they are protected against abuses of federal constitutional rights by state governments.

Adoption of the Thirteenth, Fourteenth and Fifteenth Amendments in effect constitutionalized the results of the Civil War and transformed our nation's charter. The Fourteenth Amendment in particular started us down a path to consider what rights apply to the citizens of the United States, and which might not apply (separately) to citizens of the several States. Early in American history (pre-Civil War), in *Barron v. Baltimore* (1833) the Court held (in the Fifth Amendment context), that protection of individual liberties in the Bill of Rights applied only to the federal government, and *not* to state or local governments. First, the Court argued that the Constitution and Bill of Rights were adopted by and for the people of the United States, not the several states, so its protections did not extend to the individual states. Second, the argument continued, if the Framers had intended for such application, they would have said so; and they did not. Of course, that argument was not water-tight, as not all of the ten Amendments limit themselves textually to the federal government. Further, it is troubling to us today to think that state and local governments were free to violate basic federal constitutional rights. But *Barron* made clear that *(for the moment) the Bill of Rights only applied to actions of the federal government.*

After the Civil War Amendments were ratified, the *Slaughter-House Cases* (1873) (Miller) were a false start toward extending Bill of Rights protections to actions of state and local governments. In that case, the Louisiana legislature had given a monopoly and fixed fees in the livestock slaughtering business for New Orleans to the Crescent City Livestock Landing and Slaughter-House Company. Several butchers brought suit to challenge the monopoly. They argued that the state law impermissibly violated their right to practice their trade, invoking much of the language in the recently-adopted Amendments. Among their arguments were that the law: (1) created involuntary servitude; (2) deprived them of property without due process of law; (3) denied equal protection of the law; and (4) abridged their Privileges and Immunities as citizens.

The Court narrowly construed all three Civil War Amendments and rejected the challenge to the monopoly. The majority held that the purpose of the Thirteenth and Fourteenth Amendments was to protect former slaves, only. The Amendments were interpreted narrowly so as to offer protection only to reach that goal. The Court held that the Amendments were designed to protect: "the freedom of the slave race, the security and firm establishment of that freedom, and the protection of the newly-made freeman and citizen from the oppressions of those who had formerly exercised unlimited dominion over him."[1] Further the Court held that the Privileges and Immunities Clause was *not* meant to protect individuals from state government actions and was *not* meant to be a basis for federal courts to invalidate state laws. "Such a construction. . . would constitute this court a perpetual censor upon all legislation of the States, on the civil right of their own citizens, with authority to nullify such as it did not approve as consistent with those rights, as they existed at the time of adoption of this amendment. . . . We are convinced that no such results were intended by the Congress which proposed these amendments, nor by the legislatures of the states which ratified them."[2] Thus the Privileges and Immunities Clause was removed as a basis for applying the Bill of Rights.

(The Privileges and Immunities Clause was rendered a nullity by this opinion. Since the adoption of the Fourteenth Amendment, a law been declared unconstitutional as violating the Clause only once, in *Saenz v. Roe* (1999) (Stevens). The Court invoked the Clause in the context of a California law that limited welfare payments for new residents to the level of the state from which they came. Declaring the right to travel a fundamental right, the Court held that the right to travel encompasses the right to be treated the same as longer-term residents, protected by the Fourteenth

---

1 Slaughter-House Cases, 83 U.S. 36, 71 (1872).

2 Id. at 78.

Amendment Privileges and Immunities Clause. But this is mainly an exception to what is essentially a dead area of law.)

So where are we? Let's put this in context, going back in time again, to the *Slaughter-House Cases*, where the Court rejected the attempt to establish that individual constitutional rights applied to the citizens of the States. Strike One: Pre-Civil War, *Barron v. Baltimore* held that the federal Bill of Rights apply only to the federal government. Strike Two: the *Slaughter-House Cases* read the Reconstruction Amendments very narrowly. So at this stage, the Bill of Rights provided fairly little concrete protection for the individual against actions by state and local governments. The U.S. Constitution was limited in its scope. But what changed this? *Incorporation.*

In the 1940s, 50s and 60s, in a series of Criminal Procedure cases, the Court expounded on the subject. A leading case is *Duncan v. Louisiana* (1968) (White), where the Court confronted the Sixth Amendment issue of whether a criminal defendant is guaranteed a right to jury trial in state courts. The right is explicit in the Sixth Amendment, but it had not been held to apply to the states. The majority adopted a **selective incorporation** approach. The Court held that as a matter of due process, the Fourteenth Amendment dictates that fundamental principles of liberty and justice dictate that fundamental rights essential to a fair trial must apply to state proceedings. These basics of our system of justice are fundamental constitutional rights which the Fourteenth Amendment guarantees to apply to the actions of States. "The question thus is whether given this kind of system a particular procedure is fundamental—whether, that is, a procedure is necessary to an Anglo-American regime of ordered liberty."[3] Taking one right, one issue at a time, the process of selective incorporation brought one right after another into a place where it was not only required in federal

[3] Duncan v. State of La., 391 U.S. 145, 150 n.14 (1968).

proceedings, but also in state-level proceedings. Incorporation came in a string of cases, in which the Court asked which Bill of Rights guarantees are so fundamental that as a matter of due process they applied to the states under the Fourteenth Amendment, as well as to the federal government. As a result, *virtually all federal constitutional rights have been incorporated and states are bound by the Bill of Rights, including the First Amendment* (free speech, free press, right of assembly and petition, free exercise of religion, non-establishment of religion); the Fourth Amendment (no unreasonable search or seizure); the Fifth Amendment (self-incrimination, double jeopardy, takings); the Sixth Amendment (counsel, speedy trial, confrontation); and the Eighth Amendment (cruel and unusual punishment). Incorporation is still an ongoing process. The Supreme Court recently incorporated the Eight Amendment's Excessive Fines Clause in *Timbs v. Indiana* (2019) (Ginsburg). And it is important to note that *states may provide more protection than is guaranteed by Bill of Rights, but they may not provide less protection.* The U.S. Constitution provides a floor, but it is not a ceiling on individual rights.

What's the takeaway? Certain rights are protected in the U.S. Constitution, and those protections also apply to the states. Here's a quick summary:

1. Before the Civil War, (*Barron*) the Court refused to apply the Bill of Rights against the states.

2. After the post-Civil War Amendments, an attempt to turn to the Privileges and Immunities Clause as a source of judicially implied fundamental rights against states was rejected in *The Slaughter-House Cases*.

3. Via **incorporation**, the Fourteenth Amendment Due Process Clause bars states from denying certain fundamental rights protected by the Bill of Rights.

Why do we read and discuss these materials? You will likely spend little time on this; it is a transition to make sure you understand that although we are looking at the Bill of Rights from the U.S. Constitution, the principles involved also apply to the states. And that is a transition between the structural half of the course that deals with the interplay between state and federal systems, and the individual rights half which deals with the role of the courts as the guarantors of individual rights.

CHAPTER 9

Due Process

The Fourteenth Amendment to the Constitution is central to our understanding of individual rights, as well as being at the core of a debate on how we read and interpret the great document itself. The text mandates: "[No] State [shall] deprive any person of life, liberty, or property, without due process of law."[1] In Con Law we examine what is commonly referred to as "Substantive Due Process"—examining more than the narrow question of what specific *procedures*, under the umbrella of "due process," are guaranteed by the Constitution. Substantive Due Process asks about the substance of the law itself, not the processes. The Court has often held that the Constitution contains some guarantees of *substantive rights* that are protected by the Due Process Clause of the Fourteenth Amendment. Over time, the Clause has been held to encompass many rights, including abortion, the right to die, and more. The earliest cases that dealt with Substantive Due Process examined individuals' right to contract freely and the Court deemed that individuals were allowed to do so without interference from state governments. This theory was later repudiated. Many modern cases deal with non-economic rights, and all of these cases highlight

---

1 U.S. Const. amend. XIV, § 1.

the challenges of interpreting the *meaning* of the Constitution, beyond just the limited text. In addition, there's a recurring theme of the interplay between federalism and states' rights, since we are, after all, interpreting the Fourteenth Amendment.

A. The *Lochner* Era

In the late 19th and early 20th century, the Court treated freedom to contract as a basic right under the liberty and property provisions of the Due Process Clause. In the *Lochner* era the Court aggressively protected economic rights and effectively read *laissez faire* economic values into the text of the Constitution. State laws regulating maximum hours and minimum wages were declared unconstitutional—in violation of the Fourteenth Amendment—as impermissibly interfering with the freedom to contract.

This early case law relied on a theory of *natural law*. In short, natural law theorists suggest that *a written constitution is not the beginning and end of our rights, but instead, it reaffirms a social compact that preserves and protects fundamental rights; there is some discernible* ***natural law*** *that preexists any written law. These rights deserve protection regardless of whether they are explicitly espoused in the written document.* That raises two key questions: first is whether we can assume that to be the case; and second, if so, how do we discern the specific values that are incorporated by such an approach?

These early cases embrace a theory of *laissez faire* economics—a belief that the government should allow the marketplace to operate free of regulation and intervention, and by and large should not regulate business. This theory is Darwinian: in the absence of heavy regulation, the strongest businesses thrive and the weakest ones die. As applied judicially, *laissez faire* economics was based on the belief that government regulations improperly interfered with natural rights of people to own and use their own property and labor with the freedom to contract—that is, to sell or buy one's labor.

The key case in this period is *Lochner v. New York* (1905) (Peckham). The New York law in question set maximum hours for bakery employees (10 hours/day and 60 hours/week). Lochner owned a bakery and allegedly had an employee working more than 60 hours in a week, in violation of the law. He challenged the constitutionality of that law. (Today we assume such laws to be constitutional, but that was not the case then.) The majority ruled in favor of Lochner, making three key points. First, *freedom to contract* is a basic right protected as a liberty right under the Due Process Clause. The Court held that the "statute necessarily interferes with the right of contract between the employer and employees[.] . . . The general right to make a contract in relation to his business is part of the liberty of the individual protected by the [Fourteenth] Amendment[.] . . . The right to purchase or to sell labor is part of the liberty protected by this amendment, unless there are circumstances which exclude the right."[2] Second, if there were to be any regulation of hours, a *valid "police purpose" would be necessary*, so that the government could interfere with the freedom to contract only to protect public safety, health, or morals. More specifically, it was the role of state and local governments, not the federal government, to regulate in such areas. Finally, *courts must carefully review economic regulation* to ensure that it serves a legitimate police purpose. The Court instructed reviewing courts to ask: "Is this a fair, reasonable, and appropriate exercise of the police power of the State, or is it an unreasonable, unnecessary, and arbitrary interference with the right of the individual to his personal liberty, or to enter into those labor

2 Lochner v. New York, 198 U.S. 45, 53 (1905).

contracts in relation to labor which may seem to him appropriate or necessary for the support of himself and his family?"[3]

In analyzing the New York law, the Supreme Court started from a perspective that assumed economic free will and the ability for men to bargain equally in a market: "There is no reasonable ground for interfering with the liberty of person or the right of free contract, by determining the hours of labor, in the occupation of a baker. There is no contention that bakers as a class are not equal in intelligence and capacity to men in other trades or manual occupations, or that they are not able to assert their rights and care for themselves without the protecting arm of the state, interfering with their independence of judgment and of action."[4] The Court thus invalidated the New York law as exceeding the police power.

What's the takeaway? *Lochner* invalidated, under the *substantive implications* of the Fourteenth Amendment, the New York maximum hours law for bakers. The majority held that the substantive right to contract was fundamental; it rejected government redistribution and paternalism, while finding public health to be a legitimate governmental end. Ultimately the Court held that the government's assertion that wages and hours affect health was too remote.

Why do we read and discuss *Lochner*? As you will see (spoiler alert!), the premise behind *Lochner* was ultimately repudiated. So that begs the question. We read it because it sets up our analysis of the specific meaning of the Fourteenth Amendment and larger questions of textual interpretation. There are several steps that are worth noting now, which ultimately carry forward throughout Due Process analysis and elsewhere. First, the *Lochner* opinion looked at the word "liberty" from the Fourteenth Amendment and took it to mean something more than freedom from bodily restraint. But even

---

3 Id. at 56.

4 Id. at 57.

if liberty means more than that, there is still the question of why "due process of law" means *more than* entitlement to fair *procedures.* In other words, the Court said that there is some substantive aspect to due process, which extends to some liberties beyond bodily control. But with that being the case, why would contracting be protected? Which liberties are protected? The majority relied on its sense of natural law. The Court assumed something that pre-existed the Constitution, so as to find a right to contract for—to buy and sell—one's labor. Just as important as the majority opinion is Justice Holmes' dissent, which wholly rejected the majority's premise and reliance on natural law. He argued that the Constitution should not be used to limit governmental regulation and that the Court should not promote *laissez faire* economic theory or policies. "The [Fourteenth] Amendment does not enact Mr. Herbert Spencer's Social Statics [a then-prominent exposition of Social Darwinism]. . . . a constitution is not intended to embody a particular economic theory, whether of paternalism and the organic relation of the citizen to the State or of laissez faire."[5] Fundamentally, the key question that Lochner presents to us is: *how do we find meaning in a centuries-old document with few words—what meaning can we ascribe while remaining true to the original?* It is, after all, a *constitution* we are expounding!

The end of the *Lochner* era came (perhaps not coincidentally) at the same time as President Franklin Roosevelt's ill-fated Court-packing plan and Justice Owen Roberts' *switch in time that saved The Nine* (see Chapter 4) during the era of New Deal and Depression-era politics. The pressure was on for the Court to abandon its espousal of *laissez faire* economic values; throughout the Great Depression, key thought leaders in legal, economic, and political circles across the nation endorsed the basic belief that government economic regulation was essential for the nation's recovery. With

[5] Id. at 75 (Holmes, dissenting).

rampant unemployment, the reality was that laborers had no leverage in bargaining for wages, hours, and working conditions. The country and the Court eschewed the underlying premise of *laissez faire* economics.

Lochner's demise came out of a series of cases you will study. One prime example is *Nebbia v. New York* (1934) (Roberts). The Court considered the question of whether a New York law setting minimum and maximum milk prices violated the Constitution. Given the history of the law, price fluctuations, losses of farmers, the essential nature of milk in our society, the dangers of impure milk, and the importance of milk production as a business in New York, it would have been enough to say that the milk industry sufficiently affects the public interest and therefore could be regulated. But the Court went farther. The majority opinion questioned the fundamental premise of the *Lochner* era. "[N]either property rights nor contract rights are absolute; for government cannot exist if the citizen may at will use his property to the detriment of his fellows, or exercise his freedom of contract to work them harm. Equally fundamental with the private right is that of the public to regulate it in the common interest."[6] The Court thus struck one key *Lochner* point in holding that *freedom to contract is not absolute*, and *the government may regulate in that area*. The next blow to *Lochner* came as follows: "So far as the requirement of due process is concerned, and in the absence of other constitutional restriction, a state is free to adopt whatever economic policy may reasonably be deemed to promote public welfare, and to enforce that policy by legislation adapted to its purpose. The courts are without authority either to declare such policy, or, when it is declared by the legislature, to override it."[7]

---

[6] Nebbia v. People of New York, 291 U.S. 502, 523 (1934).

[7] Id. at 537.

Three years later, in *West Coast Hotel v. Parrish* (1937) (Hughes), the Court reviewed and upheld a minimum wage law for women and expressly overruled prior *Lochner* era case law guaranteeing Substantive Due Process to contract without any governmental interference. The way in which the Court carried out its mandate was striking: "What is this freedom? The Constitution does not speak of freedom of contract. It speaks of liberty and prohibits the deprivation of liberty without due process of law."[8] The Court clarified its position and put the matter into a bigger context: "There is an additional and compelling consideration which recent economic experience has brought into a strong light. The exploitation of a class of workers who are in an unequal position with respect to bargaining power and are thus relatively defenseless against the denial of a living wage is not only detrimental to their health and well being, but casts a direct burden for their support upon the community."[9] During the *Lochner* era, the Court had refused to allow the government to regulate in order to equalize bargaining power. Now, it was permitted.

What's the takeaway? In these cases, the Court declared that it would no longer protect the freedom to contract as a fundamental right, free from governmental regulation. The Court held that in terms of economic interests, the government can regulate to serve a legitimate purpose, and the judiciary should *defer* to the legislature's choices—as long as those choices are deemed to be reasonable. And the *federal* Constitution's Fourteenth Amendment governed the actions of state and local governments. *Lochner*—as a broad statement about the protection of economic rights—was declared dead.

We have one last example of the turn that Court took: *Williamson v. Lee Optical* (1955) (Douglas). Here, the Court

---

[8] W. Coast Hotel Co. v. Parrish, 300 U.S. 379, 391 (1937).

[9] Id. at 399.

reviewed an Oklahoma law which prohibited anyone other than a licensed ophthalmologist or optometrist from fitting lenses to a face or replacing lenses without a prescription. The law was a power play by ophthalmologists and optometrists to control or shut down opticians. Showing extreme deference to the legislature, the Court upheld the law, stressing the need for judicial deference to choices made by state legislatures. "The Oklahoma law may exact a needless, wasteful requirement in many cases. But *it is for the legislature, not the courts, to balance* the advantages and disadvantages of the new requirement."[10] The opinion pondered possible (far-fetched or even silly) reasons why the state legislature enacted this law, but made clear that while the law might be illogical, in some of its applications, "[t]he day is gone when this Court uses the Due Process Clause . . . to strike down state laws, regulatory of business and industrial conditions, because they may be unwise, improvident, or out of harmony with a particular school of thought."[11] Again, *Lochner* was dead.

What's the takeaway from *Lee Optical*? In this, and other post-*Lochner* era cases, the Court may have been content to believe that the political process would work its will to balance competing economic and political interests. But they were no longer going to step in the middle of an economic fight because of a presumed freedom of contract once believed to be protected by the Due Process Clause. *So long as a reviewing court can glean some legitimate legislative purpose and so long as the law is reasonable, the challenged law will be upheld. Economic due process theory was rejected.*

Why do we read these cases that overturn *Lochner*? When teaching the Due Process Clause, I like to ask my students: *Where is*

---

[10] Williamson v. Lee Optical of Oklahoma Inc., 348 U.S. 483, 487 (1955) (emphasis added).

[11] Id. at 488.

it written? This takes us to bigger questions of constitutional interpretation. This is fundamental to your understanding of the course, and opinions here and throughout your legal career. The Constitution does not specifically address everything that can be addressed. If it did, it would be much more like a book of statutes, rather than a charter of government. So, there's a lot that is not written within it. How do we figure out what the few words that are written mean? Some (judicial formalists, or strict interpretation adherents) would say, just look to see where it's written, and if it's not in there, then it's not protected. That is appealing in its simplicity, but hardly sufficient. To say that if it isn't written it isn't protected is overly simplistic, almost mindless. Of course, there must be some sort of content that is protected that is not written; as the Court wrote in *McCulloch*, "it is a *Constitution* we are expounding."[12] But what *is* implicit in the text? Is there some sort of *natural law* or any fundamental human rights that pre-exist any written constitution, truths which are self-evident that are protected no matter what? And if so, what is the content and extent of those rights? Or do we confine our inquiry to interpreting only the words in the text? In that case, we have the same basic concern: How do we interpret a text that was written centuries ago by men who lived in a different society, all of whom are now dead? They wrote a deeply complicated document that is a beginning, not an end. As the preamble promises, we are trying "to form a more perfect Union,"[13] and naturally that means we are evolving as a society, as is our understanding of what the charter of our existence means.

As our society continues to grow and change, we must find and articulate limits on and principles to guide constitutional interpretation. The Constitution is our rock, and it must anchor us,

---

[12] McCulloch v. Maryland, 17 U.S. 316, 407 (1819).

[13] U.S. Const. Preamble.

but our interpretation cannot be frozen in time. The document doesn't change, but it governs changing problems. The problem is figuring out what our charter means. That must be done with legitimacy and consistency of method, for without that, our society would be unstable. And if the Court is not consistent and clear, then its legitimacy is undermined. Textual interpretation is hard. Many labels will be thrown out at you: strict construction, originalism, evolving constitutions, and more. Keep your mind open to understanding why every approach poses challenges, and try to find the methodology that works best for you. Be secure in your opinion, but never closed-minded about the weak spots in your case.

B. Privacy I: Reproductive Rights

Substantive Due Process asks about the substance of the law itself, not the processes. Substantive Due Process analysis asks whether the government has an adequate reason or justification for depriving or taking away a person's life, liberty, or property. When a law burdens the exercise of "fundamental rights," Substantive Due Process analysis is required to examine the law. The requirement of Due Process of law mandates not only fair *procedures* in the *application* of legal rules, but also acceptable *substance* in their *content*. In considering that question, we ask *how can we define that substance/content which is so fundamental that it merits such protection?* We also confront issues of federal-state relations, considering what guarantees are mandated by the federal constitution, to bind the states as well.

We move forward with Substantive Due Process analysis in the context of *individual rights*, and specifically the *right to privacy*. The *Lochner* era provided a debate over essential questions of whether it is proper to incorporate certain values into the text of the Constitution. In those cases, we were dealing with questions of economic theories and rights. We now consider personal rights and liberties, asking whether something extra should be read into the Constitution in order to protect individual rights.

An early pivotal case in this jurisprudence is *Griswold v. Connecticut* (1965) (Douglas). This involved a challenge to a Connecticut law that prohibited the use of contraceptives, and also punished those who assisted, abetted, or counseled such action. (The case originated in New Haven. Legend has it that in the years leading up to it, drugstores sold condoms in violation of the statute, but nobody would prosecute those "illegal" purchases, despite Yale Law professor Thomas Emerson reportedly buying condoms then pleading with police to arrest him. Imagine such a law today! Professor Emerson ended up successfully arguing the case before the U.S. Supreme Court.)

The Court struck down the law. What the Justices said is more interesting than that simple conclusion. Importantly, and quite relevant as we shall continue to see, the majority opinion did not directly embrace the due process implications. "We are met with a wide range of questions that implicate the Due Process Clause of the Fourteenth Amendment. Overtones of some arguments suggest that *Lochner* should be our guide. But we decline that invitation. . . . We do not sit as a super-legislature to determine the wisdom, need, and propriety of laws that touch economic problems, business affairs, or social conditions."[14] *So if this is not about Substantive Due Process, what is it about?* It is about fundamental rights: the majority found that *the right to privacy is a fundamental right. But where do we find this—Is it in the Bill of Rights?* The majority held that privacy is implicit in many of the specific provisions of the Bill of Rights, relying on the "penumbras" of the First, Third, Fourth, and Fifth Amendments, as had been interpreted in key cases. "The foregoing cases suggest that specific guarantees in the Bill of Rights have penumbras, formed by emanations from

14 Griswold v. Connecticut, 381 U.S. 479, 481-82 (1965).

those guarantees that help give them life and substance. Various guarantees create zones of privacy. . . . These cases bear witness that the right of privacy which presses for recognition here is a legitimate one."[15] From there, the Court concluded that the law in question violated the right to privacy of married couples—invading the marital bedroom, at least figuratively, in a way which the Fourth Amendment would prohibit if literally done by the police.

In some ways, the majority opinion was not convincing; the law clearly did not violate any of the Amendments specifically. That opinion found some right of privacy in the penumbras of the Bill of Rights—somewhere in the shadows. Although the majority opinion determined there was a right to privacy, it did not perfectly explain where that right was, beyond the penumbras. Beyond the methodology, the opinion was limited as it did not spell out an explicit right to contraception or reproductive freedom, although it did open the door for much more. In other words, while Justice Douglas' majority opinion struck down the statute as violating "marital privacy," it left many questions unanswered.

In addition to the majority, there were several concurring and dissenting opinions. The concurrence by Justice Harlan has stood the test of time better than any of the other opinions. He relied on the liberty clause and confronted the *Lochner* issue directly, arguing that *the right to privacy should be protected under the liberty of the Due Process Clause*. Harlan found the right in the Fourteenth Amendment, making specific reference to his dissenting opinion in *Poe v. Ullman* (1961) (Frankfurter). In *Poe* he wrote, "The full scope of the liberty guaranteed by the Due Process Clause cannot be found in or limited by the precise terms of the specific guarantees elsewhere provided in the Constitution. This 'liberty' is not a series of isolated points pricked out in terms of the taking of property; the freedom of speech, press, and religion; the right to keep and bear

[15] Id. at 484-85 (citations omitted).

arms; the freedom from unreasonable searches and seizures; and so on. It is a rational continuum which, broadly speaking, includes a freedom from all substantial arbitrary impositions and purposeless restraints, and which also recognizes, that certain interests require particularly careful scrutiny of the state needs asserted to justify their abridgment."[16] Harlan admitted that he was reading something into the text of the Constitution, but he argued that his approach simply gave meaning to a privacy right that even pre-dates the Bill of Rights. (Echoes of natural law, perhaps? If so, what are the parameters?) Justice Harlan argued that judicial discretion in giving content to unspecified rights could be constrained by the teachings of history, the traditions of our people, and the basic values that underlie our society.

What's the takeaway? *Griswold* declared a fundamental right to privacy, at least in the marital bedroom. (While *Griswold* was limited in its holding to protect the privacy of the marital bedroom, it was read more broadly in subsequent cases. For example, in *Eisenstadt v. Baird* (1972) (Brennan), the Court struck down a Massachusetts law that banned the distribution of contraceptives to unmarried people.) The various opinions in *Griswold* took many different paths to that conclusion, but there was a clear majority finding a fundamental privacy right somewhere in the great document.

Why do we read and discuss *Griswold*? First and foremost, it establishes a right to privacy. *Griswold* is cited continuously over the decades that follow, and it is the foundational moment of a robust interpretation of the constitutional right to privacy. What follows from there is the key question of how to define that right of privacy, the natural next step in the question of interpretation we saw earlier. A majority found a right to privacy *somewhere* in the

---

[16] Poe v. Ullman, 367 U.S. 497, 543 (1961) (Harlan, dissenting) (citations omitted).

Constitution. Its exact sources and boundaries were not clearly agreed upon. And with that emerging coalition, several justices objected to this move to interpret the Constitution more broadly, warning it was another version of *Lochner*. Justice Black, a Bill of Rights absolutist, offered a counter-point that we must consider. "I get nowhere in this case by talk about a constitutional 'right of privacy' as an emanation from one or more constitutional provisions. I like my privacy as well as the next one, but I am nevertheless compelled to admit that government has a right to invade it unless prohibited by some specific constitutional provision."[17] He bemoaned the return of the "totally discredited" *Lochner* era and railed against the importation of external philosophy into the text: "I cannot rely on the Due Process Clause or the Ninth Amendment or any mysterious and uncertain natural law concept as a reason for striking down this state law."[18] Similarly, Justice Stewart's dissent argued: "this is an uncommonly silly law. . . . But we are not asked in this case to say whether we think this law is unwise, or even asinine."[19] Agreeing with Justice Black that there is no general right to privacy, he wrote that it is not the role of the Court to second-guess legislatures, and this law was not barred by the Constitution, and that is the only question the Court should ask.

So the challenge was to determine the exact privacy right involved in *Griswold*, and moving forward through the materials we continue to discern the specific nature of the right to privacy. *Griswold* is still good law, and it still seems that there exists a constitutional privacy right, but the challenge lies in defining the dimensions. This is in large part a question of textual interpretation and the fundamental battle between competing broad and narrow

[17] Griswold, 381 U.S. at 509-10 (Black, dissenting) (footnotes omitted).

[18] Id. at 522.

[19] Id. at 527 (Stewart, dissenting).

interpretations of a two-hundred-year-old blueprint for a nation—the Constitution.

Roe v. Wade (1973) (Blackmun) is the next step in this field and a momentous case in American history, and (along with *Dobbs,* which we will discuss soon) still a rallying point on all sides of the issue today.[20] The case involved a challenge to a Texas law that prohibited all abortions, except to save the life of the mother. The companion case of *Doe v. Bolton* challenged a Georgia law that outlawed abortions, except if the doctor determined that the pregnancy would endanger the woman's life or health, if the fetus was likely to be born with a serious birth defect, or if the pregnancy resulted from rape. By now, you already know that the Court held that *the Constitution protects the right of a woman to choose to terminate pregnancy prior to viability (the time at which the fetus can survive outside the womb).*

You basically knew that already, right? We must nonetheless consider how and why the Court reached that conclusion. The answer is found again in the Due Process Clause and is fundamentally about privacy. The majority opinion first traced the history of abortion then moved into the legal analysis, discussing the right to privacy as developed in *Griswold* and related cases. The Court pronounced the following about privacy and abortion: "This right of privacy, whether it be founded in the Fourteenth Amendment's concept of personal liberty and restrictions upon state action, as we feel it is, or, as the District Court determined, in the Ninth Amendment's reservation of rights to the people, is broad enough to encompass a woman's decision whether or not to terminate her pregnancy."[21] The right of privacy was not found within the Bill of Rights' penumbras as declared in the *Griswold*

---

[20] Note that we will discuss *Dobbs* soon after *Roe*; even though *Dobbs* overruled *Roe* and *Casey*, those cases are still important for our understanding in this field.

[21] Roe v. Wade, 410 U.S. 113, 153 (1973).

majority opinion, but instead in the Due Process Clause. The Court then explained why prohibiting abortion infringes on a woman's right to privacy, concluding that forcing a woman to keep and bear a child against her will imposes tremendous physical, mental, and societal burdens. Accordingly, the Court held that a woman must be allowed to make the choice. But that decision is not free at all times and under all circumstances.

Having established a right to privacy which encompasses the right to choose to terminate pregnancy, the Court considered when, why, and how the state could infringe upon the right. The Court explained that *the right to an abortion is not absolute and that it must be balanced against other considerations, such as the state's interest in protecting the potential life*. In a nutshell, it balanced the various interests at play.

The foremost consideration concerned the fetus as a developing human life. Importantly, *the Court did not find that the fetus was a "person" meriting constitutional protection*. This portion of the decision was grounded in interpretation of the Constitution, which did not indicate the possibility of such intention ("the word 'person,' as used in the Fourteenth Amendment, does not include the unborn."[22]). Plus, the opinion surveyed religious, philosophical, and other teachings, noting the great disagreement as to the question of when life begins. The Court's conclusion: "We need not resolve the difficult question of when life begins. When those trained in the respective disciplines of medicine, philosophy, and theology are unable to arrive at any consensus, the judiciary, at this point in the development of man's knowledge, is not in a position to speculate as to the answer. . . . The unborn have never been recognized *in the law* as persons in the whole sense."[23] Having held that a fetus is not, constitutionally speaking, a person, the

[22] Id. at 158.

[23] Id. at 159, 162 (emphasis added).

question remained: *What interest can the state have if not in protecting the life of an unborn fetus?* In balancing interests, the Court held that the state has a compelling interest in protecting two things:

1. maternal health after the first trimester
2. the potential of human life after viability

In the end, how could states regulate abortion under Roe*?* The Court divided pregnancy (for legal purposes) into three trimesters. During the first trimester, the government could not prohibit abortions and could regulate them only as it regulated other medical procedures. During the second trimester, the government could not ban abortions, but it could regulate in ways that are reasonably related to maternal health. Post-viability, which the Court determined to be during the third trimester, the government could prohibit abortion except if necessary to preserve the life or health of the woman.

What's the takeaway? The Court held that *the Constitution protects the right of a woman to choose to terminate pregnancy prior to viability, which is the time at which the fetus can survive outside the womb* (usually around the end of the second trimester). More specifically, the Court held that *the government may not prohibit abortions prior to viability and that government regulation of abortion had to meet strict scrutiny.*[24]

Why do we read and discuss *Roe*? As you probably already know (not exactly a spoiler alert), *Roe* has been overturned. Nonetheless, *Roe* leads to so many questions, and the core one is about constitutional interpretation and the question: *Where is it written?* The *specific* right to an abortion is neither mentioned in the text nor explicitly addressed by the Framers. If you spend all day looking, you will never find the words abortion or pregnancy in

[24] We discuss levels of scrutiny in Chapter 11.

the Constitution. What does it mean that they didn't say anything about it? Some argue that since it is not mentioned in the text, then the right does not exist. But what about other rights the Court has read into text—is this not as important as the right to marry, to procreate, etc.? This debate reflects a much broader question of how courts should interpret the Constitution and when, if ever, it is proper for the Court *to protect unenumerated rights*. In this context, the Court found a right to privacy within the Fourteenth Amendment and held that the privacy right encompasses a woman's right to choose to terminate pregnancy.

Roe also is such a big case, with countless layers. While still keeping things short and happy, there are a few other points I want to raise about *Roe*, dealing with what it did not do. It's worth noting that:

- It can be argued that the Court gave short shrift to the state's interest in protecting fetal life. I challenge you to think about what interest that may be. Did the Court correctly decline to decide when life begins? Arguably yes, since there are simply too many choices and none is absolutely correct. And even if a fetus is deemed a person, can we as a society force a woman to be an incubator against her will—why force one person to use her body to save another? But there's still a question about when life begins. The Court said that it need not decide when life begins, but, in the end, didn't it really decide? Arguably, it only decided that *the Constitution* does not provide rights for a fetus.
- The Court could have decided this on Equal Protection grounds, not Due Process. After all, this is about *women* who are pregnant, and only women can become pregnant. That would not solve the

fundamental problem, but it would have shifted the analytical framework, moving outside of the privacy context. The hard questions would still remain, but the Court overlooked the question, and you should consider it (and we will talk about Equal Protection in Chapter 11).

- Ultimately, perhaps this is all just an *unsatisfactory compromise*, and an all or nothing approach would have been better. Both sides were disappointed, because while it established a woman's right to choose, that right can be restrained; likewise, while the Court established the state's interest in protecting potential life, that too is constrained.

Since *Roe*, there were many efforts to overturn it: through the amendment process, in legislatures, and in courts. We will soon discuss *Dobbs*, which overruled *Roe*, but in the near-50 years in between, there's much to discuss about the attacks on *Roe* and its analytical approach. The discussion illuminates important aspects of constitutional interpretation. The constitutional amendment process did not succeed, but many laws restricted the availability of abortions and court challenges ensued through the '70s and '80s, leading up to the monumental 1992 decision, *Planned Parenthood of Southeastern Pennsylvania v. Casey* (O'Connor/Kennedy/Souter). The Pennsylvania law in question restricted access to abortions in various ways, including requiring informed consent, waiting periods, and parental and spousal notification. Again (no major spoiler alert), *Casey* was overruled in *Dobbs*, but it is important to study and discuss.

First, you will see that this is what I call a "scorecard" opinion: where you almost need a scorecard to keep track of who wrote for what sort of majority or other coalition, who concurred (in whole or part), who dissented (in whole or part), and ultimately who "won." Here, we see five opinions divided along three basic lines:

- O'Connor-Souter-Kennedy (for the Court, but also for a plurality), reaffirming *Roe* in the abstract, but also allowing most of these restrictions on the exercise of the right to stand;
- Blackmun and Stevens, completely reaffirming *Roe*; and
- Rehnquist and Scalia (joined by White and Thomas), who would overrule *Roe*.

The triumvirate's opinion began with a broad declaration: "Liberty finds no refuge in a jurisprudence of doubt."[25] From there the Court held that, based on (1) principles of institutional integrity and (2) the rule of *stare decisis*, the "essential holding of *Roe v. Wade* should be retained and once again reaffirmed."[26] *What does that mean?*

- A woman has a personal/privacy right to choose to have an abortion in the period before viability without undue interference from the state;
- The state has an interest in the fetus, such that it may restrict abortions as long as any law has exceptions for pregnancies that endanger the woman's life or health; and
- The state has an interest in the woman's health and fetal health.

The opinion developed in a series of parts, making these key points. First and foremost, the opinion is about Due Process, privacy, and *Roe*. The opinion reaffirmed, based on *Roe*, that *the*

---

[25] Planned Parenthood of Se. Pennsylvania v. Casey, 505 U.S. 833, 844 (1992).

[26] Id. at 846.

Due Process Clause has a substantive component, rejecting any argument to the contrary: "It is a promise of the Constitution that there is a realm of personal liberty which the government may not enter."[27] The Court continued later, "It is settled now, as it was when the Court heard arguments in *Roe v. Wade*, that the Constitution places limits on a State's right to interfere with a person's most basic decisions about family and parenthood, as well as bodily integrity."[28] Second, the opinion recognized that abortion is a unique act. Despite a history and culture that has perceived a vision of the woman's role as mother, "[h]er suffering is too intimate and personal"[29] for the government to insist on a woman's acceptance of this role. Third, the Court reviewed the importance of *Roe* in American society and the American legal framework, and by applying principles of *stare decisis*, explained why *Roe* should not be overruled, but must instead be reaffirmed. The foundations of *Roe* were solid, a body of case law had followed applying the decision, and countless individuals have relied on that case's explication of privacy rights. The Court concluded that it could not repudiate *Roe*'s underpinning: a constitutional liberty interest that a woman possesses to control her reproductive rights and, consequently, the right to choose to terminate pregnancy. So *Roe* was upheld.

Here's the twist. Even while upholding the "core" of *Roe*, the Court rejected *Roe*'s trimester framework, "which we do not consider to be part of the essential holding of *Roe*."[30] The Court came up with a new analytical method. The new framework from *Casey* is as follows: the state may not place *undue burdens* on the right to choose to terminate pregnancy pre-viability. A law is unduly burdensome if it "has the purpose or effect of placing a substantial

---

[27] Id. at 847 (citations omitted).
[28] Id. at 849 (citations omitted).
[29] Id. at 852.
[30] Id. at 873.

obstacle in the path of a woman seeking an abortion of a nonviable fetus."[31]

This was a split decision. *Roe* was upheld, albeit with a new standard involving undue burdens and substantial obstacles. An apparent victory for proponents of abortion rights. But the Court also upheld most of the restrictions on abortions that had been challenged. The Court sustained most of Pennsylvania's law, allowing regulations requiring informed consent, extra notice requirements, a 24-hour waiting period, and additional record-keeping, but rejected spousal consent as unduly burdensome. An apparent victory for opponents of abortion rights. In other words, the legal core of *Roe* stood, but Pennsylvania's restrictions on abortions were largely upheld.

What's the takeaway? *Casey* was a step along the line toward *Dobbs* (but not going nearly as far as *Dobbs*, as we will see). On the one hand, the decision affirmed the Court's previous holding that a woman has a constitutionally-protected right to choose to terminate pregnancy, as part of a broad right to bodily privacy implicitly found in the Due Process Clause. On the other, the Court limited the right but still held that the state may not place any undue burdens—as defined by the Court—on the exercise of that right, meaning it may not place any substantial obstacles in the way.

Why do we read and discuss *Casey*? While *Casey* has since been overruled, it provided a definition of the nature of the privacy right involved in abortion, and also revealed a deep-seated divide over several issues that are central to analyzing and understanding Constitutional Law: how to interpret the Constitution; the meaning of the Due Process Clause; the specific meaning of *Roe*; and the importance of *stare decisis*. The opinion very deliberately opens with the sentence "Liberty finds no refuge in a jurisprudence of

---

31 Id. at 877.

doubt."[32] The Court was playing a role as the protector of individual rights. In that context, the Court declares rights, and people rely on those declarations. Inconsistency from the Court—a jurisprudence of doubt—can make individuals uncertain as to their rights and their liberty would be undermined. This question is front and center going forward, into the *Dobbs* decision.

Put another way, as elected officials enact laws, the courts stand ready to ensure that individual rights are protected. And specifically, the Court sees its role in protecting liberty beyond just *declaring* what rights exist, but also in ensuring that those rights are continuously and consistently protected. Thus the Court is reading the Constitution in a flexible, non-technical manner, elaborating on the meaning of the Due Process Clause. The big fight was over the essence of *Roe* and overturning it. A majority specifically voted to uphold *Roe*, albeit with a split as to exactly what is at *Roe*'s core. But a dissenting group was livid that the Court did not overturn it. The central O'Connor-Kennedy-Souter trio held the cards. As they explained, if the Court were to overturn *Roe,* then that would destabilize the nature of the right to choose to terminate pregnancy. That liberty/right would be meaningless if there was a body of constantly changing case law—a jurisprudence of doubt. The majority argued that *Roe* should be reaffirmed, not overturned, consistent with principles of *stare decisis*. The argument was that *Roe* has not been proven unworkable; it had been relied on for decades, and "No evolution of legal principle has left *Roe*'s doctrinal footings weaker than they were in 1973."[33] To overrule *Roe* not only would destabilize the individual right, but it would also undermine the legitimacy of the Court and call into question the rule of law. This concept and these words were both prophetic and essential to our understanding of what comes next.

---

[32] Id. at 844.

[33] Id. at 857.

For nearly five decades *Roe* and *Casey* defined this discussion, with the declaration of a right, but a constant re-examination of the parameters of that right, and in 2022 these two cases were decisively overruled in *Dobbs v. Jackson Women's Health Org.*[34] The case involved a challenge to a 2018 Mississippi law that banned most abortions after the first 15 weeks of pregnancy. Jackson Women's Health Organization was Mississippi's only abortion clinic at the time, and they brought legal action against the state department of health and various individual officials, seeking to enjoin the law. Applying *Casey*, the federal district court enjoined the law's enforcement. The Fifth Circuit Court of Appeals affirmed, and the case was then appealed to the U.S. Supreme Court. The Court upheld the validity of the Mississippi law, overruling *Roe* and *Casey*.

The Court explored the broader question of the meaning of the Due Process Clause and how to interpret its scope; analyzed the specific question of whether there is a constitutionally protected right to an abortion; and expounded on the meaning and importance of *stare decisis*.

The primary question was whether the Constitution, in the Due Process Clause, protects a woman's right to choose to terminate pregnancy. In discussing the Due Process Clause, the Court spelled out what is now the definitive analytical approach, employing the framework from *Washington v. Glucksberg* (1997) (discussed toward the end of this chapter). The key inquiry is to "examine whether the right at issue . . . is rooted in our Nation's history and tradition."[35] That involves an inquiry into the text and the history, asking what was understood at the time the specific provision of the Constitution was drafted and ratified. Without explicit language, and without a finding that such a right is essential to our Nation's scheme of ordered liberty, the Court's "inescapable conclusion is that a right

---

[34] 597 U.S. 215 (2022).

[35] Id. at 234.

to an abortion in not deeply rooted in the Nation's history and traditions." The Court's analysis was further informed by it's inquiry finding that abortion was criminalized under common law and statutory criminal law through much of the nation's history.

Further, the Court addressed *stare decisis,* as it rejected *Roe* and its progeny. The majority found fundamental flaws in *Roe*, holding that "*Roe* was egregiously wrong from the start,"[36] and there was insufficient reason to uphold it, further opining that *Casey* simply reaffirmed *Roe* solely based on *stare decisis*. Since *Roe* wrongly found that the Constitution protected the right to abortion, *Casey* couldn't stand. The Court concluded: "We therefore hold that the Constitution does not confer a right to abortion. *Roe* and *Casey* must be overruled, and the authority to regulate abortion must be returned to the people and their elected representatives."[37] In other words, there is no constitutional protection, and states (and Congress) may regulate and restrict abortions as they choose, through the political process.

Chief Justice Roberts concurred in the result only, somewhat characteristically seeking a less dramatic middle ground. He emphasized his disagreement with *Roe*, but he argued that "there is a clear path to deciding this case correctly without overruling *Roe* all the way down to the studs: recognize that the viability line must be discarded, as the majority rightly does, and leave for another day whether to reject any right to an abortion at all."[38]

Concurring, Justice Thomas took issue with the majority's apparent limitations on the opinion and its application elsewhere. He wrote: "in future cases, we should reconsider all of this Court's substantive due process precedents, including *Griswold*, *Lawrence*,

---

[36] Id. at 231.

[37] Id. at 292.

[38] Id. at 353 (Roberts, concurring).

and *Obergefell*."[39] Justice Kavanagh tried to refute that argument in his concurrence.

Justice Breyer dissented, joined by Justices Kagan and Sotomayor. His main argument can best be found in this language: "This Court has rejected the majority's pinched view of how to read our Constitution. 'The Founders,' we recently wrote, 'knew they were writing a document designed to apply to ever-changing circumstances over centuries.' Or in the words of the great Chief Justice John Marshall, our Constitution is 'intended to endure for ages to come,' and must adapt itself to a future 'seen dimly,' if at all. That is indeed why our Constitution is written as it is. The Framers (both in 1788 and 1868) understood that the world changes. So they did not define rights by reference to the specific practices existing at the time. Instead, the Framers defined rights in general terms, to permit future evolution in their scope and meaning. And over the course of our history, this Court has taken up the Framers' invitation. It has kept true to the Framers' principles by applying them in new ways, responsive to new societal understandings and conditions."[40]

The dissent also challenged the majority's historical argument on its own terms, refuting the central Due Process Clause analysis and outcome. Further, the dissenters took aim at the majority's approach to *stare decisis*, calling into question the majority's entire analysis, writing, "No recent developments, in either law or fact, have eroded or cast doubt on those precedents. Nothing, in short, has changed. Indeed, the Court in *Casey* already found all of that to be true. *Casey* is a precedent about precedent. It reviewed the same arguments made here in support of overruling *Roe*, and it found that doing so was not warranted. The Court reverses course today for

---

[39] Id. at 332 (Thomas, concurring). (We will discuss *Lawrence* both later in this chapter and in Chapter 11, and *Obergefell* in Chapter 11.)

[40] Id. at 374 (Breyer, dissenting (citations omitted)).

one reason and one reason only: because the composition of this Court has changed."[41] He found it to be cold comfort that the majority returned the question to the states, as these restrictions curtail the freedom of American women.

In addressing the open question of what might come next, as addressed by Justice Thomas and perhaps refuted by Justice Kavanagh, the dissent concluded: "we cannot understand how anyone can be confident that today's opinion will be the last of its kind."[42]

What's the takeaway? *The Constitution does not confer a right to abortion; Roe and Casey are overruled; and the authority to regulate abortion is returned to the people and their elected representatives in the states.*

Why do we read and discuss *Dobbs*? This case is the continuation of perhaps the most widely debated and discussed issue of constitutional law in the last 50+ years. It is important in our politics and society at large, as well as in our study of Constitutional Law. In the latter context, the opinion provides significant limits on substantive due process rights and in many ways marks the triumph of originalism. This marks the ascendance of what the majority calls a historical approach, and also perhaps as Justice Breyer said, the result of changing personnel on the Court, and a decision illuminating the meaning of *stare decisis*.

C. Privacy II: Bodily Rights

We now look at a small batch of case law dealing with other individual rights over one's body, specifically, dealing with (1) private sexual conduct (and homosexuality); and (2) death and dying.

---

[41] Id. at 364.

[42] Id. at 386.

Sexual Relations

First, we explore privacy rights under the Due Process Clause involving sex and sexual relations. In *Bowers v. Hardwick* (1986) (White) the Court upheld a Georgia law that banned the act of sodomy, defined to include anal or oral sex. The majority rejected the argument that the specific sex act fell within the sphere of privacy that the Court had delineated in *Griswold*, *Roe*, et al., and it was protected: "[W]e think it evident that none of the rights announced in those cases bears any resemblance to the claimed constitutional right of homosexuals to engage in acts of sodomy that is asserted in this case."[43]

Less than twenty years later, the Court reexamined the issue in *Lawrence v. Texas* (2003) (Kennedy). While this case was specifically about the question of the right of adults to engage in private consensual sexual conduct, the core issue was *liberty*. The opinion began: "Liberty protects the person from unwarranted government intrusions into a dwelling or other private places. In our tradition the State is not omnipresent in the home. And there are other spheres of our lives and existence, outside the home, where the State should not be a dominant presence. Freedom extends beyond spatial bounds. Liberty presumes an autonomy of self that includes freedom of thought, belief, expression, and certain intimate conduct. The instant case involves liberty of the person both in its spatial and in its more transcendent dimensions."[44] But the question was what to do about the precedent in *Bowers*. The Court's answer: We need to reconsider. The opinion traced a string of cases, starting with *Griswold*, then moving through *Roe*, and others, observing that "The statutes do seek to control a personal relationship that, whether or not entitled to formal recognition in the law, is within the liberty of persons to choose without being

---

[43] Bowers v. Hardwick, 478 U.S. 186, 190-91 (1986).

[44] Lawrence v. Texas, 539 U.S. 558, 562 (2003).

punished as criminals."[45] It is a bond, and "[t]he liberty protected by the Constitution allows homosexual persons the right to make this choice."[46] Looking back at *Bowers* and also at *Casey* and *Romer v. Evans* (dealing with sexual orientation in the Equal Protection context—we'll get to that in Chapter 11), the Court concluded that *Bowers* could not stand. The Court emphasized the importance of *stare decisis*, but also observed that it is not an inexorable command. *Bowers* was overruled, and the Texas law was declared unconstitutional.[47]

What's the takeaway? Individuals have a right to privacy, firmly rooted in the Fourteenth Amendment Due Process Clause. That includes the right to engage in consensual sex acts, for same-sex acts or opposite sex. The state cannot ban "homosexual sodomy." (Note also that there are Due Process considerations in our discussion of same-sex marriage, in Chapter 11.)

Why do we read and discuss *Lawrence v. Texas*? At its core is a debate over how to interpret the Constitution, and how individual rights are protected, even against a potentially unfriendly majority sentiment. Justice Scalia, dissenting, argued that the law in question was firmly rooted in our history (see *Glucksberg*, and now *Dobbs*), and that it is acceptable for society to criminalize conduct we find immoral. "Today's opinion is the product of a Court, which is the product of a law-profession culture, that has largely signed on to the so-called homosexual agenda, by which I mean the agenda promoted by some homosexual activists directed at eliminating the moral opprobrium that has traditionally attached to homosexual conduct. . . . [T]he Court has taken sides in the culture war, departing from its role of assuring, as neutral observer,

[45] Id. at 567.

[46] Id.

[47] Interestingly, in 1990, after he had retired, Justice Powell publicly commented "I think I probably made a mistake in that one," referring to his being the deciding vote in *Bowers*, a 5-4 opinion.

that the democratic rules of engagement are observed."[48] (I find it interesting that when I teach this dissent, my students (who run the political gamut) see this as puzzlingly anachronistic. To the current generation, Scalia's underlying premise, and the perspective of the dissent itself, is almost laughable, and even bigoted. But the challenge I put to them, and to you, is to address the merits of his underlying legal argument.) Scalia saw this as a political battle that has gone one way, and argued that it's not the Court's role to intervene. But the majority saw it as being about individual rights, and in our system, the Court's most important role is to stand up for individual rights when the legislative majority is acting to restrain those rights. Justice Kennedy's opinion observed that modern times "show an emerging awareness that liberty gives substantial protection to adult persons in deciding how to conduct their private lives in matters pertaining to sex."[49] And he saw the Constitution not as a static document frozen in time. "As the Constitution endures, persons in every generation can invoke its principles in their own search for greater freedom."[50] **This is about the role of the Court as the protector of individual rights in our democracy.**

So we come full circle, back to the fundamental question of what is the nature of privacy, what are the parameters of constitutionally-guaranteed privacy rights, and what are the proper sources for answering these questions? *Where is it written?* If the Court is going to construe the Constitution to contain fundamental rights that aren't explicitly declared in the document itself, then it needs to be careful that the rights it is protecting reflect some substantial consensus. But the increasing diversity of our country makes moral consensus an almost unworkable ideal. There will always be accusations of "*Lochner*izing" from some segment of the population. Answering the core question of interpretation demands

[48] Lawrence v. Texas, 539 U.S. 558, 602 (2003) (Scalia, dissenting).

[49] Id. at 559.

[50] Id. at 579.

as clear an answer as possible, if the Court is to serve as the ultimate protector of individual rights.

Right to Die

The last discussion in this area is the so-called right to die. You are too young to remember Nancy Cruzan, a young woman who was in a car accident and ended up in a persistent vegetative state, sustained by a feeding tube. Her family sought to withdraw the feeding tube, which eventually would lead to her death. The situation captured national attention, and ultimately the legal case went to the U.S. Supreme Court in *Cruzan v. Missouri Department of Health* (1990) (Rehnquist). In the decision, the Court assumed that there was a right to decide to refuse medical treatment, which would lead to death. But how could someone choose to exercise that right, and who could make such a decision if the person, like Nancy Cruzan, was unable to speak for herself? That was a sort of evidentiary question—what would be sufficient to prove that it was someone's true wish, in essence, to die? The Court upheld Missouri's standard of proof required to exercise the right (in this case, clear and convincing evidence when involving an incompetent individual). (This topic also was very much in the news particularly in the 1990s, with Jack Kevorkian in Michigan, a.k.a. "Dr. Death.")

The Court took a next step in *Washington v. Glucksberg* (1997) (Rehnquist), reviewing a Washington state prohibition against "causing" or "aiding" suicide. The concern raised by the parties was that the Due Process Clause encompasses a liberty interest in controlling the time and manner of one's death, and the State may not interfere. To resolve this issue, the Court applied a test based upon our Nation's history and traditions

The Court noted that "the Due Process Clause specifically protects those fundamental rights and liberties which are, objectively, 'deeply rooted in this Nation's history and tradition.' "[51] Rehnquist believed that "[o]ur Nation's history, legal traditions, and practices thus provide the crucial 'guideposts for responsible decision making,' that direct and restrain our exposition of the Due Process Clause."[52] Simply put, *Glucksberg* demands that the fundamental right being protected must be one that is deeply rooted in tradition and history. However, plaintiffs may not claim broad rights such as a right to bodily autonomy; instead, there must be "a 'careful description' of the asserted fundamental liberty interest."[53] In *Glucksberg*, this meant that the question was limited to whether or not there was history or tradition of recognizing "a right to commit suicide with another's assistance."[54]

In applying this test, the Court responded that historically it always has been a crime to assist suicide, and that it had been reaffirmed recently. This demonstrated that there was neither history nor tradition of a right to assisted suicide. Chief Justice Rehnquist acknowledged that the Due Process Clause includes liberty, including the right to refuse unwanted treatment (from *Cruzan*). He added that to define liberty interests the Court looks at its roots, and the concept of ordered liberty. Looking at precedent, the Court observed that *Cruzan* dealt with refusing unwanted medical treatment, which this was not. This was seen as an affirmative act to end life, as compared to refusing medical treatment. On the other hand, the state had an interest in preserving human life, and an interest in protecting vulnerable groups. With those considerations they found no violation of a Due Process liberty interest.

---

[51] Washington v. Glucksberg, 521 U.S. 702, 720-21 (1997) (quoting Moore v. City of E. Cleveland, Ohio, 431 U.S. 494, 503 (1977)).

[52] Id. at 721 (quoting Collins v. City of Harker Heights, Tex., 503 U.S. 115, 125 (1992)).

[53] Id. (quoting Reno v. Flores, 507 U.S. 292, 302 (1993)).

[54] Id. at 724.

What's the takeaway? *Glucksberg* further defines the parameters of the liberty interest first identified in *Cruzan*, and it asks whether that liberty interest encompasses assisted death. The Court did not declare physician-assisted suicide to be a constitutionally protected right.

Why do we read and discuss this material? It wraps up the discussion on privacy and liberty, and again brings in the question of balance. While there are numerous privacy rights we have explored, the state also has competing interests to look out for. So here, as with the abortion cases, we ask, *what is the state's interest in life?* How should the state interest be weighed against a competent, terminally ill person's liberty interest if that person is experiencing unremitting pain, for example? And if we recognize a constitutionally protected right to assisted death, what are the parameters there?

In sum, these last materials add to the reproductive rights cases, further defining where the individual's privacy rights begin and when/whether/how the state has an interest in intervening.

CHAPTER 10

State Actions and the Beginnings of Constitutional Law

A. State Action

This brief chapter explores a fundamental principle of how and where the protections of the Amendments apply—*the Constitution generally does not apply to private entities or actors.* Statutes may govern private conduct, but the Constitution's protections of individual liberties and the Equal Protection mandate apply *only* to governmental action. In principle this may sound simple, but it is not so easily implemented. Laid out in the late nineteenth century, the doctrine has degenerated, but I will do my best to present it to you in a short and happy way!

We start with the *Civil Rights Cases* (1883) (Bradley). The Fourteenth Amendment had been ratified in 1868, and Congress had followed with the Civil Rights Act of 1875, mandating that all persons are entitled to full and equal enjoyment of accommodations, advantages, facilities, and privileges of inns, public conveyances on land or water, theaters, and other places of public amusement. The law prohibited *private* race discrimination and provided both civil and criminal penalties for violations. It would appear to fit in well with the post-Civil War mandate. But the Court held the Act to be unconstitutional, reasoning that the Fourteenth Amendment applied to governmental actions, *not* to private conduct. Thus, circa 1875, the Constitution itself offered no protection against private wrongs, no matter how discriminatory or how much they infringed upon individual rights. Justice Harlan's dissent voiced a different perspective: "I cannot resist the conclusion that the substance and spirit of the recent amendments of the Constitution have been sacrificed by a subtle and ingenious verbal criticism."[1] He instead referred broadly to the *purpose* of the Amendment and reached the conclusion that the Constitution enabled Congress to prohibit private discrimination in public transportation and accommodations.

Having established the baseline premise that private actors are not covered by/included under the Fourteenth Amendment, now we consider where and why that premise does *not* apply. The Court has held that in some circumstances, private entities are engaging in **state action** and are therefore subject to the constraints of the Fourteenth Amendment. There are two big conceptual areas for exploration: *(1) the public function strand and (2) the nexus strand.* Many cases discuss the various strands and sub-strands almost interchangeably, but we will sort it all out.

Public Function Strand

We start with the *public function* strand, which looks at ways in which private actors might be subject to constitutional constraints because they have somehow taken on a public function. *Marsh v. Alabama* (1946) (Black) is the seminal case, using the context of a company town and management of private property to explain the public function rationale. A company owned the town

[1] Civil Rights Cases, 109 U.S. 3, 26 (1883).

where it operated, and the land where its employees lived. Even though a private company owned the streets of the company town, the Court found that the company was subject to constitutional constraints as it carried out those functions of running the town. This was because the company town was in all respects like a public town, only with title to the land held in private hands. In the *White Primary Cases* (a series of cases dealing with whites-only voting restrictions in primary elections—*Nixon v. Herndon* (1927), *Nixon v. Condon* (1932), *Grove v. Townsend* (1935), *Smith v. Allwright* (1944), and *Terry v. Adams* (1953)), the Court again found a private entity taking on a public function. The Court held that voting in primaries was such an exclusive traditional government function that private political parties could not escape the mandates of the Constitution. So, if a private entity takes on a public function, the state action doctrine holds that the private entity may be subject to constitutional constraints, as though it were a governmental entity.

Nexus Strand

Next we consider state involvement and the *nexus strand* of the state action doctrine. In *Shelley v. Kraemer* (1948) (Vinson), homes were sold to black families where there were racial covenants in place that banned blacks from living in the homes. Neighbors sued to prevent the new owners from taking possession of the properties they had purchased. State courts enforced those restrictions, postulating that the covenants were purely private agreements that "ran with the land" and were enforceable against subsequent owners. The question was *could courts enforce private contracts whereby members of a neighborhood agreed not to sell their property to blacks?* The argument in favor of the racial covenants was that private contractual agreements need not comply with the Constitution, and court enforcement was simply implementation of private choices. Even though the Court reiterated the basic state action principle that limits the reach of the Fourteenth Amendment, nonetheless state action was found. Through court enforcement (state involvement), the government facilitated the discrimination. "These are not cases. . . in which the States have merely abstained from action. . . . Rather, these are cases in which the States have made available to such individuals the full coercive power of government to deny to petitioners, on the grounds of race or color, the enjoyment of property rights. . ."[2] Enforcement of private race discrimination by the courts in essence was state action, and therefore a public role governed by the Constitution.

But what are the limits? State action cannot be found based on just **any** government involvement. A few cases illustrate these limitations. *Burton v. Wilmington Parking Authority* (1961) (Clark) involved a sit-in protest in a privately owned diner located in a municipal parking structure. The parking structure had been built with knowledge of and need for the restaurant and accompanying revenue. The Court held: "By its inaction, the Authority, and through it the State, has not only made itself a party to the refusal of service, but has elected to place its power, property, and prestige behind the admitted discrimination. The State has so far insinuated itself into a position of interdependence with [the restaurant] that it must be recognized as a joint participant in the challenged activity."[3] Thus, the *involvement* or *entanglement* between the state and the private company dictated that state action was implicated in the unconstitutional deprivation of individual rights.

It is not enough simply to have just any involvement; instead it must be involvement to a *significant extent*. For example, in *Moose Lodge v. Irvis* (1972) (Rehnquist), the Court expanded on the

---

[2] Shelley v. Kraemer, 334 U.S. 1, 19 (1948).

[3] Burton v. Wilmington Parking Auth., 365 U.S. 715, 725 (1961).

relationship required between the state and the private acts and actors, restricting the reach of the state action requirement. There, the Court confronted a situation where a private club in Pennsylvania that received a liquor license as part of a state regulation of clubs, discriminated against blacks. The Court found that although similar *governmental* action would be prohibited under the Fourteenth Amendment, there was no state action when a private club denied service to an individual because of his race. On its way to a conclusion, the opinion acknowledged that private ownership is not determinative in the matter, but without some state involvement, there would be no constitutional implications. Instead of allowing for a finding of state action whenever there was any state involvement, like a liquor licensing scheme, the opinion instead observed: "[o]ur holdings indicate that where the impetus for the discrimination is private, the State must have *significantly involved* itself with invidious discriminations, in order for the discriminatory action to fall within the ambit of constitutional prohibition."[4] The net effect is that *something more is required, something like a significant nexus, not just between the state and the private actor, but also between the state and the allegedly unconstitutional act, before the Court will find state action.*

Another example comes in another case you will likely read, *Jackson v. Metropolitan Edison Co.* (1974) (Rehnquist). Jackson had her electric service cut off, and she argued that it was done without constitutionally-required due process. The utility was privately operated and claimed that there was no constitutional requirement of due process, because it was not a state actor. So the question became *whether a private utility, operating under a state-granted monopoly, had to provide due process before terminating a customer's service.* In finding *no state action*, the Court observed: "The mere fact that a business is subject to state regulation does

[4] Moose Lodge No. 107 v. Irvis, 407 U.S. 163, 173 (1972).

not by itself convert its action into that of the State for purposes of the Fourteenth Amendment. Nor does the fact that the regulation is extensive and detailed, as in the case of most public utilities, do so."[5] The court was not moved by the company's monopoly status, the way it carried out an apparent public function, and the state's authorization and approval of the termination procedure in question. Instead, the Court treated the company as *only* a heavily regulated private utility, thus not subject to constitutional due process concerns. Since that time, in most cases, state action typically is not found, reflecting a vision on the part of the Court that the doctrine is to be employed sparingly.

The narrow view of state action has continued, as seen in *Manhattan Community Access Corporation v. Halleck* (2019) (Kavanaugh). Halleck was barred from submitting her film to a privately owned public access channel. The Court held that the operation of a public access channel was not a state action and was therefore not subject to the First Amendment. The Court narrowly interpreted the doctrine, observing: "[i]t is not enough that the federal, state, or local government exercised the function in the past, or still does. And it is not enough that the function serves the public good or the public interest in some way. Rather, to qualify as a traditional, exclusive public function within the meaning of our state-action precedents, the government must have traditionally and exclusively performed the function."[6] The Court's limited and fact-bound analysis was heavily influenced by its view of the history of regulation in this area: "operating public access channels on a cable system is not a traditional, exclusive public function within the meaning of this Court's cases."[7]

---

5 Jackson v. Metro. Edison Co., 419 U.S. 345, 350 (1974).

6 Manhattan Cmty. Access Corp. v. Halleck, 587 U.S. 802, 809 (2019).

7 Id. at 811.

What's the takeaway, and why do we discuss state action? The doctrine fundamentally affirms a principle that the Constitution governs only the actions of the state, and those playing a public role with significant state enforcement. It may be easy to find state action in most lawsuits, if the state acts directly on a private party, for example. But that is the easy case. The hard cases—the conceptual disaster area—arise when a nominally private party is charged with depriving someone of equal protection, due process, or some other constitutional right. The case law is often inconsistent. More than anything, this reflects a fundamental concern with the question of how far the Court should reach and how far it should withhold. The recent trend is toward a narrow view of the scope of the doctrine. A formal view of the text insulates much quasi-public activity committed by theoretically private actors.

B. Section 5 Civil Rights Enforcement Power

The Reconstruction Amendments provide that "Congress shall have power to enforce this article by appropriate legislation."[8] In the context of *Dred Scott* and the Civil War, the Amendments shifted the balance of power toward the federal legislative branch, Congress. But what is the scope of this congressional power under the Thirteenth, Fourteenth and Fifteenth Amendments? The key question is whether Congress is limited to providing *remedies* for violations of constitutional rights as defined by the U.S. Supreme Court, or does Congress have some independent interpretation powers? This involves defining the meaning of the words "to enforce" and "appropriate legislation." These questions are in some ways more like structural issues than individual rights issues. We briefly look at two competing views of the answer, in *Katzenbach v. Morgan* (an expansive view), and *City of Boerne v. Flores* (a

[8] U.S. Const. amend. XIII, § 2; id. amend. XIV, § 5; id. amend. XV, § 2.

restrictive view). The prevailing view is that Congress' power is *limited to remedies that are "proportionate and congruent" to remedying or preventing state violations of Court-declared rights.*

In *Katzenbach v. Morgan* (1966) (Brennan) the Court reviewed Section 4(e) of the Voting Rights Act of 1965. In a previous case, *Lassiter*, the Court had upheld as constitutional an English language literacy requirement for voting. Congress subsequently enacted Section 4(e) of the VRA in part explicitly to challenge and reject *Lassiter*. The specific section in question contained an English language literacy provision that allowed for Puerto Ricans educated through the sixth grade to pass automatically. Congress wrote a rule that was arguably contrary to the *Lassiter* decision. The question became, *does Congress have the power to do this*—was it a proper exercise of Section 5 of the Fourteenth Amendment, "to enforce, by appropriate legislation, the provisions of this article."[9] The Court held that this was a proper exercise of the Section 5 enforcement power. The Court held that Congress may independently interpret the Constitution and even, in effect, overturn the U.S. Supreme Court. *Why?* First, the Court held that Congress could have concluded that granting Puerto Ricans the right to vote would empower them and help combat discrimination against them—it was a *remedial law* within congressional power to protect the guarantees of the Fourteenth Amendment. Second, Congress could find that the literacy test itself denied Equal Protection—even though that would be contrary to *Lassiter*. Justice Brennan's analysis: "By including Section 5 the draftsmen sought to grant to Congress, by a specific provision applicable to the Fourteenth Amendment, the same broad powers expressed in the Necessary and Proper Clause."[10]

---

[9] U.S. Const. amend. XIV, § 5.

[10] Katzenbach v. Morgan, 384 U.S. 641, 650 (1966).

What's the takeaway from *Katzenbach v. Morgan*? Congress can use its Section 5 enforcement power to *independently* interpret the Constitution. More specifically, it does not give Congress the power to determine the substance of the Constitution, but it does allow Congress to "ratchet up" the protections provided therein due to its interpretation.

From that point in the 1960s, the Court has turned toward a more restrictive view of the scope of congressional enforcement power under Section 5, as exemplified in *City of Boerne v. Flores* (1997) (Kennedy). In *Employment Division v. Smith* (1990), the Court had enunciated a new standard for analyzing free exercise (religion) cases. The Religious Freedom Restoration Act (RFRA) was a direct challenge to that decision, with Congress spelling out its contrary view of the proper standard for analysis. Local zoning authorities denied a Texas church a permit to build a new facility because the old one was a historic landmark. The church sued under the RFRA and the City in turn challenged RFRA's constitutionality. The Court held that under Section 5, Congress may not create new rights or expand the scope of rights. Congress is limited to laws that *prevent* or *remedy* violations of rights recognized by the Court. "Congress' power under Section 5 . . . extends only to 'enforcing' the provisions of the Fourteenth Amendment. The Court has described this power as 'remedial'."[11] In other words, Congress may not determine the substance of the Constitution. Otherwise, the Court argued, the Supreme Court would no longer be in the position *Marbury* carved out, nor would the Constitution occupy the same special place. "If Congress could define its own powers by altering the Fourteenth Amendment's meaning, no longer would the Constitution be 'superior, paramount law, unchangeable by ordinary means.' It would be 'on a level with ordinary legislative acts, and like other acts, alterable when the legislature shall please to alter

[11] City of Boerne v. Flores, 521 U.S. 507, 519 (1997).

it.' "[12] Here, RFRA was found unconstitutional because it impermissibly expanded the scope of rights and was not proportionate or congruent as a preventative or remedial measure. "RFRA is so out of proportion to a supposed remedial or preventive object that it cannot be understood as responsive to, or designed to prevent, unconstitutional behavior. It appears, instead, to attempt a substantive change in constitutional protections."[13]

What's the takeaway? Congress may not create new rights or expand the scope of existing rights pursuant to its Section 5 authority. Congress is limited to laws that *prevent* or *remedy* violations of rights recognized by the Court.

Why do we read and discuss *Morgan v. Katzenbach* and *City of Boerne*? There is a central philosophical discussion about the role of the different branches here—it is both about civil rights enforcement and the separation of powers. The current view, as embraced in *City of Boerne*, protects the role of the Court as the authoritative interpreter of the meaning of the Constitution, arguably protecting the Constitution as the Great Document itself. It also fits in with a vision of a limited federal government/legislative branch, along the lines of other cases like *Lopez*, and it restricts the reach of Congress to address Fourteenth Amendment violations. In some ways, we can see it to be similar to the power grabs we saw in the very early cases, like *Marbury* and *McCulloch v. Maryland*. The earlier approach to Section 5 viewed the Constitution as setting a floor upon which the legislature could add, providing more power for Congress and giving fuller meaning to Section 5. It provided a view that the federal Congress should have broader power. The current prevailing view holds that the federal government is more limited in enforcing the equality commands of the Fourteenth Amendment. The U.S. Supreme Court

---

[12] Id. at 529.

[13] Id. at 532.

thus restrains the coordinate federal legislative branch and simultaneously protects the states. In sum, while some have argued that Section 5 gives broad authority to Congress to enact prophylactic legislation beyond Court interpretations of the Fourteenth Amendment, the Court has made clear that *Section 5 is limited to remedies "proportionate and congruent" to remedying or preventing state violations of Court-declared rights.*

CHAPTER 11

Equal Protection

A. Equal Protection and Tiers of Scrutiny

The Constitution, as originally drafted, had no provisions ensuring equal protection under the law. This may be obvious, considering that women were disenfranchised and routinely discriminated against and that blacks were legally held as slaves. However, after the Civil War, Congress ratified the Fourteenth Amendment with its promise that "No state shall deny. . . to any person the equal protection of the laws."[1] Despite that command, little changed for nearly 100 years, largely because of Jim Crow laws. *Brown v. Board of Education* (1954) ushered in the modern era of Equal Protection analysis, paving the way for the Equal Protection Clause to be used to combat discrimination and to protect fundamental rights.

As with Due Process, in this analysis of the Equal Protection Clause we will be searching for meaning in a small number of words. In the Equal Protection context, we have a structured analysis, starting with a main inquiry: *whether the government's classification of individuals under the law is justified by a sufficient*

1 U.S. Const. amend. XIV.

purpose. Many laws draw lines and thus could be susceptible to Equal Protection challenges under a broad reading of the Equal Protection Clause. For example, think about age requirements for getting a driver's license. It makes sense that five-year-olds shouldn't drive; some age minimum is clearly appropriate, but what is the right age is not perfectly clear. In that situation, there is clearly a classification, and for constitutional purposes we ask whether it is justified. How? By looking at the government's objective in classifying—or discriminating. Depending upon the type of classification, *different levels of scrutiny* will be employed to decide whether the classification is constitutional—***strict scrutiny, intermediate scrutiny, or rational basis review.***

We can most usefully break down Equal Protection analysis into three questions.

1. What is the classification?
2. What is the appropriate level of scrutiny?
3. Does the governmental action survive the appropriate scrutiny?

Question 1: Classification

Equal Protection analysis always starts by identifying *how* the government is distinguishing among people. *What is the government's classification*? The answer to this question is not always clear, but there are two basic ways to arrive at a solution. The first is to look for *facial classifications, which are found in the very text of the law*. These draw a distinction among people based on a particular characteristic. This classification exists on the face of the law; one can understand the classification simply by reading the text of the law. . . Examples: only white men serving on juries; only those aged 16 and older eligible for driver's licenses. The greatest concern arises when the classification involves immutable characteristics—those things we cannot change about ourselves.

Second, some laws are *facially neutral,* but there is a ***discriminatory impact*** *from the law* or there are *discriminatory effects of its administration.* For example, a regulation mandating all police officers to be at least 5'9" tall includes at least half of men but only a small percentage of women. This is a facially neutral law that has a discriminatory gender-based impact. But discriminatory impact alone is insufficient to prove a race or gender classification. *If a law is facially neutral, demonstrating a potentially improper race or gender classification requires proof that there is some* ***discriminatory purpose*** *behind the law.*

Question 2: Scrutiny

Once the classification has been determined, the appropriate level of scrutiny must be identified. *Different levels of scrutiny will be applied depending upon the classification.* Three levels or tiers of scrutiny are used:

Strict. *Discrimination based on race or national origin is subject to strict scrutiny.* Under strict scrutiny a law must be proven to be *necessary (narrowly tailored) to achieve a compelling government purpose.* The government has the burden of proof to show that it cannot achieve its goals through any less discriminatory alternative.

Intermediate. Intermediate scrutiny is most notably used for *discrimination based on gender.* (However, the Justices are not all in agreement on what this means or how it works.) Under intermediate scrutiny, a law is upheld if it is *substantially related to an important government purpose.* A court need not find the government's purpose compelling, but it must be *important.* The means used by the law need not be necessary, but they must bear a *substantial relationship* to the ends being sought. The burden of proof again remains on the state.

Rational Basis. Rational basis review is the minimum level of scrutiny that all laws must meet. Under rational basis review, a law will be upheld if it is *rationally related to a legitimate government purpose*. The government's ends need not be compelling or important, and the means need not be necessary or substantially related to the end. We are simply looking for a legitimate end and rational means. And the challenger (not the government) bears the burden of proof under rational basis review. It is *enormously deferential to the government,* and only rarely do courts declare laws unconstitutional for failing to meet this level of review.

The Court has been reluctant to add classifications to particular levels of scrutiny, but several criteria are employed in determining the appropriate level of scrutiny. First, the Court has emphasized that *immutable characteristics*—race, gender, national origin, and marital status of one's parents—warrant heightened (strict or intermediate) scrutiny. *Why?* It is seen as unfair to penalize someone for characteristics that the person didn't choose and/or can't change. Second, *a history of discrimination against the group* is relevant. A related factor is the court's judgment concerning the likelihood that the classification reflects naked prejudice as opposed to a permissible government purpose.

Question 3: Does the Government Action Meet (Survive) the Level of Scrutiny?

This third question is all about the fit. Having identified the classification and the corresponding level of scrutiny, we turn to *application*. In determining constitutionality under the Equal Protection Clause, the Court looks at both ends and means. *If strict scrutiny is employed, there must be a very close fit. If intermediate scrutiny, a close fit still is necessary, but it is a bit looser; and only a very loose fit is necessary if the Court is employing rational basis review.*

And now, a quick word on *over- and under-inclusiveness*, which relates to the question of *fit*. A law is under-inclusive if it does not apply to individuals who are similar to those to whom the law does apply; if it applies to one, it should apply to all. A law is over-inclusive if it sweeps in and applies to those who need not be included in order for the government to achieve its stated purpose. An example of both can be found in the internment of Japanese-Americans during World War II. It was under-inclusive because if the goal was to isolate those who were a threat to society, locking away *only* Japanese-Americans didn't make sense, as surely people of other national origins could have posed a security threat under the order's logic. It was over-inclusive because so very few Japanese-Americans posed any specific threat. The fact of over- or under-inclusiveness is not dispositive. Virtually all legal classifications are one, or the other, or both. Yet, courts use the concepts in evaluating the means-ends fit.

In sum, ask:

1. What is the classification?
2. What level of scrutiny should be applied?
3. Does the governmental action meet the level of scrutiny?

With this background, we will look at the way the analysis works under different classifications, and then we will consider remedies, including affirmative action. Finally, we will explore the fundamental interests branch of Equal Protection analysis, specifically turning to voting rights.

All this talk about levels of scrutiny reminds me of the conversations you hear about instant replay in sports. The question in these cases is *what to do with the original call made on the field—what do we presume about its correctness?* In the Equal Protection context, the courts review the original decision made in the legislative process to create some sort of classification among people. The level of scrutiny is the key question—*what do we presume about its constitutionality*? Invariably in sports replays, there's some sort of language like "incontrovertible evidence needed to overturn the original call." The instant replay review in the booth shows some level of deference to the judgment call made on the field. Levels of scrutiny simply are about deference, and in the legal context the classification dictates the level of scrutiny.

B. Strict Scrutiny and Race Cases

Race-based classifications are most likely to receive strict scrutiny. First, we look at *facial classifications* based on race, where the law on its face—by its very terms—draws a distinction among or between people based on certain characteristics. The quick starting point in the case law is *Plessy v. Ferguson* (1896) (Brown). In this case, a Louisiana statute required "separate, but equal" facilities for whites and "coloreds." In a decision that has now been discredited, the Court upheld the law as constitutional. The Court theorized that the different races were *simply* receiving separate facilities, but of equal caliber. Its central premise was: "We consider the underlying fallacy of the plaintiff's argument to consist in the assumption that the enforced separation of the two races stamps the colored race with a badge of inferiority. If this be so, it is not by reason of anything found in the act, but solely because the colored race chooses to put that construction upon it."[2] The Court held that there was no constitutional problem with race-based segregation. Justice Harlan's dissent argued that certain laws were passed to keep blacks out and establish the racial superiority of whites. "But in view of the Constitution, in the eye of the law, there is in this country no superior, dominant, ruling class of citizens. There is no caste here. Our Constitution is color-blind, and neither

---

2 Plessy v. Ferguson, 163 U.S. 537, 551 (1896).

knows nor tolerates classes among citizens. In respect of civil rights, all citizens are equal before the law. The humblest is the peer of the most powerful."[3] Still, that was merely the dissent, and the Court subsequently reaffirmed separate but equal in a number of different contexts.

Now we fast forward a couple of generations to *Brown v. Board of Education* (1954) (Warren), a seminal case in American history. The road to *Brown* was paved by a long series of cases from 1938 to 1954. In those cases, under well-developed facts, the Court found that states denied equal protection by failing to provide equal educational opportunities for blacks that were available to whites, often in the context of legal education. In these pre-*Brown* cases, the Court was invited to overturn *Plessy* but declined. In the culmination of a historical legal effort (largely spearheaded by a rising legal star Thurgood Marshall), the Court granted cert. in the 1952-53 term in five cases challenging the separate but equal doctrine in the context of elementary and high school education. Factually speaking, the cases presented starkly unequal schools. For example, the white schools had dramatically lower student-teacher ratios than the black schools, and the white schools were solidly built brick and stucco buildings with indoor plumbing compared to the black schools made of rotting wood with outhouses.

You already know the result here: a unanimous decision holding that *separate but equal was impermissible in the realm of public education.* The Court did not rule on the basis of the egregious facts alone. Instead of a narrow attack on the clearly unequal factual situation, the Court defined the issue as "the effect of segregation itself on public education," thereby opening the door for a much broader prescription from the Court.[4] The central premise of the

---

[3] Id. at 557 (Harlan, dissenting).

[4] Brown v. Bd. of Ed. of Topeka, Shawnee County, Kan., 347 U.S. 483, 492 (1954).

opinion was that state-mandated segregation inherently stamps black children as inferior and impairs their educational opportunities. "To separate them from others of similar age and qualifications solely because of their race generates a feeling of inferiority as to their status in the community that may affect their hearts and minds in a way unlikely ever to be undone."[5] *How did the Court decide that?* The Court relied heavily on psychological literature showing that segregation causes black children to feel inferior and interferes with their learning. In the end, the Court held "that in the field of public education the doctrine of 'separate but equal' has no place. Separate educational facilities are inherently unequal."[6]

What's the takeaway? *Brown* overruled *Plessy* and held that separate schools were not equal in the eyes of the Constitution. State-imposed race-based segregation was unconstitutional. Racial integration of public schools had to begin "with all deliberate speed."[7]

Why do we read and discuss *Brown*? It sets the stage for us as we consider the meaning of race and equality. Nearly two centuries after the nation was born with a constitution that accepted slavery, and nearly a century after the Civil War and the Amendments codified a new compact, the Court opened the door for a robust protection of equality with its ruling in *Brown*. The core question is *what value(s) does the Fourteenth Amendment protect?* Absolute race neutrality? Protection of one race over another? No race-based discrimination (however that is defined)? There are several possible answers. *Brown* made a clear pronouncement, but as we will see, the case law has gotten more complex and the debate over the

---

[5] Id. at 494.

[6] Id. at 495.

[7] Brown v. Bd. of Ed. of Topeka, Shawnee County, Kan., 349 U.S. 294, 301 (1955).

meaning of *Brown* and its values are in dispute now more than ever. We'll get to all that soon.

(One other note about how the Court works and about the background of this specific decision: Having heard oral argument during the 1952 Term, the Court was supposedly divided 5-4 for reaffirming separate but equal and for giving the states some time to equalize the facilities. But the case was not decided then. In the summer of 1953, Chief Justice Vinson died of a heart attack and Pres. Eisenhower appointed Earl Warren to fill the vacancy. Legend has it that after re-argument in the fall of 1953, Warren personally persuaded each Justice to join the decision overturning separate but equal.)

The next case we discuss is *Loving v. Virginia* (1967) (Warren). This was a challenge to Virginia's anti-miscegenation law, a statute that prohibited interracial cohabitation and marriage. In 1958, an interracial couple living in Virginia got married in Washington, D.C., in violation of Virginia's statute (and yes, their last name actually was Loving). The law on its face applied to both whites and blacks—neither could marry someone of the other race. The only possible precedent came in 1883's *Pace v. Alabama*, where the Court upheld a law that provided harsher penalties for adultery and fornication if it involved a white and a black person than if both were of same race. The Court was in somewhat new post-*Brown* territory, faced with this Virginia statute that did not require separate facilities.

The *Loving* Court "reject[ed] the notion that mere 'equal application' of a statute containing racial classifications is enough to remove the classifications from the Fourteenth Amendment's proscription of all invidious racial discriminations."[8] Then the Court placed a very heavy burden on the state: "The fact that Virginia prohibits only interracial marriages involving white persons

[8] Loving v. Virginia, 388 U.S. 1, 8 (1967).

demonstrates that the racial classifications must stand on their own justification, as measures designed to maintain White Supremacy. We have consistently denied the constitutionality of measures that restrict the rights of citizens on account of race. There can be no doubt that restricting the freedom to marry solely because of racial classifications violates the central meaning of equal protection."[9] Not only was there a classification, but the Court also found an invidious/discriminatory motive behind the law and struck it down.

Facial Discrimination—Racially Discriminatory Purpose and Effect

We have seen where a statute by its terms draws lines based on race, but that's not always the case. In circumstances *without* facial discrimination, what makes a statute unconstitutional? In order to answer, we engage in various levels of scrutiny, asking about the means-ends relationship—the *fit* between the classification and the government's interest. We ask whether there is some other problem—i.e., whether there is a disproportionate *impact*. Some laws that are facially neutral are administered in a manner that discriminates against a class of people or has a disproportionate impact.

The Court has held that there must be proof of a discriminatory purpose *on top of (in addition to)* discriminatory impact in order for such laws to be subjected to heightened scrutiny. A very early example came in *Yick Wo v. Hopkins* (1886) (Matthews), involving a facially neutral law administered in a discriminatory fashion. A San Francisco ordinance required that laundries be located in brick buildings unless a waiver was obtained from the Board of Supervisors, via petition. The law was racially neutral, but its application was not. Over two hundred petitions filed by Chinese-Americans had been denied, and all but one of the petitions filed by

---

[9] Id. at 11-12.

non-Chinese-Americans was granted. Those facts established a pattern of administration that was directly discriminatory against a class of people based on national origin that was ruled illegal. The Court explained: "Though the law itself be fair on its face, and impartial in appearance, yet, if it is applied and administered by public authority with an evil eye and an unequal hand, so as practically to make unjust and illegal discriminations between persons in similar circumstances, material to their rights, the denial of equal justice is still within the prohibition of the [C]onstitution."[10] Thus the ordinance as applied denied equal protection and violated the Constitution. The question remains, *How to find proof of such purposeful discrimination?*

The Court later clarified that *discriminatory impact, alone, is insufficient to prove that a facially neutral law constitutes improper classification.* Our key case is *Washington v. Davis* (1976) (White). Here, applicants for the Washington, D.C. police force were required to take a test to get the job, and statistics revealed that blacks failed the test at a much higher rate than whites. Because this was one of the main reasons why black applicants got the job at a lower rate than whites, the plaintiffs argued that the use of the test was unconstitutional. The Court rejected that argument and instead held that *proof of a discriminatory* ***impact*** *is insufficient, by itself, to show the existence of a suspect racial classification and ultimately a constitutional violation*. While this information is relevant when deciding a case, it is not constitutionally sufficient. *Laws that are facially neutral as to race and national origin will be stricken/receive heightened scrutiny only if there is proof of a discriminatory purpose (in addition to the impact).*

What's the takeaway from *Washington v. Davis?* Proof of discriminatory impact alone is not sufficient to prove an equal

[10] Yick Wo v. Hopkins, 118 U.S. 356, 373-74 (1886).

protection violation. There must also be proof of a discriminatory purpose.

Why do we read and discuss this? The Court argued that the Equal Protection Clause is designed to prevent official *conduct* discriminating on the basis of race—bad conduct, perhaps, but not unequal results alone. So that gets to one of our core questions about Equal Protection doctrine: *What equality does the Constitution "care" about: process/laws or outcome/results?* Your answer will likely also answer the question: *Should discriminatory purpose be constitutionally required, as the Court held?* Arguably yes, because:

- Equal protection is about stopping discriminatory acts of the government, not bringing about equal results;
- Too many laws would fail otherwise, because in some way they have a discriminatory impact;
- Laws can/will be written to counterbalance any unequal results, as the people see fit (through their elected officials).

On the other hand, requiring proof of discriminatory intent should *not* be required because:

- Requiring a higher level of proof insulates laws too much on evidentiary grounds. Higher burdens of proof make evidence-gathering too much of a barrier in the way of exposing constitutionally-improper behaviors;
- Racism and sexism are constant undercurrents that are almost impossible to prove;
- Our nation's long societal history of prejudice and discrimination should result in a presumption;

- Equal protection should be concerned with results, not just motivations.

In sum, we are asking big questions. To get a greater understanding of Con Law, your task is to consider all the possible answers and the associated analysis. And my task is to help you understand these issues. . . in a short and happy way.

The Benign Use of Racial Criteria: Affirmative Action

In the last couple of pages, I asked what the Equal Protection Clause is designed to protect. We continue with the central inquiry: Does the Constitution forbid state laws that *remedy* past discrimination? Alternatively, does the Constitution guarantee blacks (or other racial minorities) any particular position or place in society (results), or is it solely about ensuring a fair *process*? We will look at several cases, starting with the 1978 decision in *Regents of the University of California v. Bakke* (1978) (Powell). The University of California-Davis Medical School had designed a "special admissions program" to assure the admission of certain minorities. Bakke, a white man, challenged this system, claiming that the admissions program violated the Equal Protection Clause.

At the core of this case is the question of *what reasons would justify a governmental program to aid students based on race?* The University argued that it would be permissible to use this admissions program to reduce the historic deficit of minorities in medical schools. The Court rejected that argument because it would be inappropriate to create a race preference, if not specifically remedying a past specific discriminatory practice. Another option was to support the program in order to broadly counter societal discrimination. While the Court said that may be acceptable, there were insufficient findings to support that justification in this instance. Another alternative was to increase the population of nonwhite medical students, in order to improve the delivery of healthcare to underserved communities. The Court rejected this reason as an insufficiently compelling government interest. However, the Court was persuaded by the argument that it would be constitutionally permissible to employ some sort of race-based admissions program *in order to achieve a diverse student body*. The Court accepted that but found that the University had not met its burden of proof in that regard. So, in the end, the Court endorsed what was called the "Harvard model", where race is used as *a* factor in admissions but not as *the* factor. The UC-Davis model was held to be unconstitutional because admission hinged too exclusively on race.

What's the takeaway? Race-based programs are subject to strict scrutiny. Race can be a factor in university admissions, based on the Harvard model, where race is *a* factor but not *the* deciding factor in the evaluation of a particular student.

Why do we read and discuss *Bakke*? First, it is a key case in this area, setting up much that follows. In laying the foundation, it raises key issues that persist. First, of course, there's a question of language, perhaps semantics. Various terms are used to describe the program in UC-Davis and elsewhere, including *affirmative action, benign discrimination, race-conscious remedies, and reverse discrimination*. The terms that are used reflect underlying attitudes toward these programs.

The key holding subjects affirmative action programs like those in *Bakke* to the same level of analysis—strict scrutiny—as in *Brown*. The modern interpretation question is whether a white medical school applicant is in the same position as the black school children in *Brown*. Obviously, the two cases are in a very different position relative to each other—a generation and a world apart. But are they occupying the same constitutional ground? That is the key question. The next step is to weigh the concepts of *invidious vs. benign* line-drawing. *Why should programs designed to help minorities that previously have been subjected to discrimination be held to the same strict scrutiny as programs that have discriminated against those same minorities?* Some answers include:

- The Constitution is color blind;
- Legally speaking, racism in any form or direction is outlawed;
- We can address and remedy *specific instances of racism* with race-based laws;
- It may not make sense to make whites (like Mr. Bakke) "pay" if they "didn't do anything wrong";
- The Equal Protection Clause only guarantees *fair process*, not any specific outcome or result.

On the other hand,

- The Constitution is not really color blind;
- Despite our best intentions, racism still persists in society;
- The *results* of a long history of race-based discrimination need to be overcome—we are still a society with great disparities that cut along race lines;
- Affirmative action is qualitatively different, as minorities are being helped not hurt;
- The Equal Protection Clause guarantees *equality* of outcomes/results.

Those key points are the heart of the debate in this area. If you want to do well in Con Law (I got your attention, huh!), try to answer these questions while addressing these points. Don't try to get *the* answer or prove your point (yet), just understand and engage these questions, both here and in the classroom.

We now move out of the educational sphere for a minute to a series of cases dealing with race-based affirmative action in the hiring and contracting arena. First came *Fullilove v. Klutznick* (1980) (Burger) that upheld a federal 10% set-aside plan for construction projects, which showed deference to Congress. (Set-aside programs allow government entities to designate purchases and contracts to be bid by businesses owned by socially and economically disadvantaged individuals, often women and minorities.) In 1989, the Court shifted in *Richmond v. J.A. Croson Co.* (1989) (O'Connor), rejecting a 30% set-aside program in Richmond, Virginia for certain public construction projects that was modeled on the federal program approved in *Fullilove*. The Court observed that while in Richmond there was a "sorry history of both private and public discrimination," there was an inadequate factual basis for the city's specific program.[11] The Court subjected the program to very rigorous review, and it perceived the program as too sloppy and not well-tailored to the task. It did not survive heightened scrutiny.

Then came *Adarand v. Peña* (1995) (O'Connor), a challenge to a federal program granting preferences to economically and socially disadvantaged individuals with a presumption based on race ("[t]he contractor shall presume that socially and economically disadvantaged individuals include Black Americans, Hispanic Americans, Native Americans, Asian Pacific Americans, and other minorities").[12] Mountain Gravel, a contractor for a highway construction project, rejected Adarand's low subcontractor bid in favor of a higher bid from Gonzalez, pursuant to the federal regulations. Adarand had submitted the lowest bid but Gonzales had been certified as a disadvantaged business, so Mountain Gravel

---

[11] City of Richmond v. J.A. Croson Co., 488 U.S. 469, 499 (1989).

[12] Adarand Constructors, Inc. v. Pena, 515 U.S. 200, 205 (1995) (alteration in original).

awarded the subcontract to Gonzales due to financial incentives in its federal contract. Adarand claimed an Equal Protection violation.

The Court first addressed the question of what standard to employ when reviewing state and local programs, holding that *strict scrutiny must be applied to federal affirmative action or remedial programs* (that classify on the basis of race). **Why?** Several major themes recur from prior case law, with a two-fold emphasis: (1) skepticism of race-based classifications; and (2) a position on the question of benefits vs. burdens, or race neutrality. Notably, the Court rejected the idea that there is a *difference between benign and invidious classification/discrimination* that should justify a different type of review and instead adhered to a principle of *consistency* as a hallmark. *"Federal racial classifications, like those of a state, must serve a compelling governmental interest, and must be narrowly tailored to further that interest."*[13] That means the program has a high bar to clear, but it does not mean that the program is automatically rejected—the scrutiny is strict but not necessarily fatal in fact. The case was remanded for further proceedings consistent with the standard set forth.

Why do we read and discuss *Adarand*? An important dimension to this case is the issue of whether there is a difference between so-called benign and invidious discrimination. It is important to read *Adarand* and the related materials to consider both the distinction between the two ideas, as well as the Court's approach to the subject. The Court rejects the idea that there is a difference, but what does that mean? Certainly, a law that *prohibits* an individual from having equal access based on race—no blacks at water fountains for example—is different from a law that seeks to *help* those who have been discriminated by such laws in the past. Justice Stevens' *Adarand* dissent argues that invidious and benign are fundamentally different—just as oppression and assistance are

[13] Id. at 234 (emphasis added).

different. Is he right? Maybe, on a factual or non-legal basis he is; the motivation is different. But even if so, *does the Constitution care?* The *Adarand* majority's reply: constitutionally speaking, there is no difference. Or even more simply, *the Constitution doesn't care.*

The next stop on our tour of Equal Protection takes us back to education in companion cases in 2003: *Grutter v. Bollinger* (2003) (O'Connor) and *Gratz v. Bollinger* (2003) (Rehnquist). They involved admissions criteria at the University of Michigan, for law students and for undergrads.

First, let's look at *Grutter.* The highly selective Michigan Law School used race as a factor in admissions, seeking diversity to help enrich the education of all students. The policy was committed to racial and ethnic diversity, especially in regard to groups that have historically faced discrimination. The idea was to use that system until there was a "critical mass" of students from such underrepresented groups. Justice O'Connor applied strict scrutiny, requiring a compelling government interest to justify any government program that classifies on the basis of race. According to the Court, the Law School "assert[ed] only one justification for their use of race in the admissions process: obtaining 'the educational benefits that flow from a diverse student body.' "[14] Ultimately showing deference to the Law School's educational judgment, the Court was persuaded by this justification: "[T]he Law School has a compelling interest in attaining a diverse student body," and "attaining a diverse student body is at the heart of the Law School's proper institutional mission."[15]

The Court approved the concept of a "critical mass" because it was not "outright racial balancing," which would have been constitutionally impermissible. The Court noted several goals as

[14] Grutter v. Bollinger, 539 U.S. 306, 328 (2003).

[15] Id. at 328-29.

appropriate for such a plan: a critical mass could (1) help cross-racial understanding; (2) improve classroom dynamics and discussions; (3) lead to better learning outcomes; and (4) prepare students for a diverse workforce and society. The question remained about the fit between the government interest and the means chosen to accomplish those ends. Justice O'Connor instructed that strict scrutiny must be "flexible, nonmechanical" and should be achieved without strict racial quotas.[16] The Court instructed that the Law School could consider race as a "plus" factor (see *Bakke*, Harvard)—*a* factor, but not *the* factor.[17] "Narrow tailoring does not require exhaustion of every conceivable race-neutral alternative. . . . [It does] require serious, good faith consideration of workable race-neutral alternatives that will achieve the diversity the university seeks."[18] And this plan survived strict scrutiny.

In *Gratz,* the University of Michigan undergraduate admissions office used a variety of factors to make decisions in selecting their incoming class. They employed a 150-point scale, with 100 points needed for admission. The point structure accounted for grades and standardized tests as well as geography, athletics, and many other factors. Members of underrepresented racial or ethnic minority groups received an automatic 20 points. The Court held that while in *Grutter* they had just accepted diversity as a compelling rationale to justify race-based admissions, this method did not meet the means—it was "not narrowly tailored to achieve the interest in educational diversity that respondents claim justifies their program."[19] The fit wasn't right—not narrowly tailored to meet the compelling government interest in achieving diversity in the classroom. The Michigan Undergraduate admissions office had argued that it would be too burdensome to do a *Grutter*-like review

[16] Id. at 334.

[17] Id.

[18] Id. at 339.

[19] Gratz v. Bollinger, 539 U.S. 244, 270 (2003).

for all cases (perhaps to come closer to the Harvard model), but the Court rejected that argument, saying that this possible burden did not make the unconstitutional system constitutional.

What's the takeaway? In this *Grutter-Gratz* split decision, the Court held that race-based admissions programs are constitutional to the extent that they are trying to achieve diversity in education and using race as *one* factor but not *the* factor that determines admission. The Court held one program (the Law School) to be constitutional but struck down another (the undergraduate program). The one that survived was more amorphous. (Interestingly, when numbers are clearly introduced, the Justices seem to get a bit queasy.)

Why do we read *Grutter* and *Gratz*? The two cases provide the answer for what justifies the use of race in university admissions, and this discussion opens a wider door into the basic question of how long and under what circumstances the Constitution permits such programs. In her majority opinion in *Grutter*, Justice O'Connor approved the Michigan Law School plan, but with an interesting caveat: "race-conscious admissions policies must be limited in time."[20] *How long?* I don't know, nor do I think there is a definitive answer, but there does seem to be a 25-year timeline presented in the past cases. *Brown* was decided in 1954; *Bakke* nearly a quarter-century later in 1978, and *Grutter* and *Gratz* exactly 25 years after that. In apparent colloquy with O'Connor, Justice Ginsburg concurred in *Grutter*, "However strong the public's desire for improved education systems may be, it remains the current reality that many minority students encounter markedly inadequate and unequal educational opportunities."[21] In a sense, she seemed to be saying that while some "equality" *may be* achieved one day, that time is not now. And dissenting in *Gratz*,

---

[20] Grutter v. Bollinger, 539 U.S. 306, 342 (2003).

[21] Id. at 346 (Ginsburg, concurring) (citations omitted).

Ginsburg wrote: "But we are not far distant from an overtly discriminatory past, and the effects of centuries of law-sanctioned inequality remain painfully evident in our communities and schools."[22] With that perspective, she dissented, arguing that the Constitution *does* permit predominantly race-based admission.

Justices Souter and Scalia provide one other interesting point for you. Justice Souter dissented in *Gratz* that the undergraduate system was more like the factor approach used in *Grutter* than the quota approach condemned in *Bakke*. "Equal protection cannot become an exercise in which the winners are the ones who hide the ball."[23] While Souter, in arguing that both were permissible, was disgruntled that the two results seemed inconsistent, Scalia weighed in with a similar complaint but argued that both were *un*constitutional ("The Constitution proscribes government discrimination on the basis of race.").[24] He argued that these two decisions are a mess and only prolong the agony of inconsistent programs, with apparently inconsistent results.

Another case to consider briefly is *Parents Involved v. Seattle School Dist.* (2007) (Roberts), involving school districts that voluntarily adopted student assignment plans that used race in determining student placement in order to achieve racial balance. The question was whether a public school system could classify students based on race. Again, the Court employed strict scrutiny when analyzing a race-based school placement program. Here, the Court held that race was *the* factor—like *Gratz* not *Grutter*. Further, as to the claim that there is a benefit to a racially-integrated environment, the Court replied that, even if so, the system was *not narrowly tailored* because it was tied to the demographics of the

---

[22] Gratz v. Bollinger, 539 U.S. 244, 298 (2003) (Ginsburg, dissenting).

[23] Id. (Souter, dissenting).

[24] Grutter v. Bollinger, 539 U.S. 306, 349 (2003) (Scalia, dissenting).

area, not pedagogic needs. "[R]acial balance is not to be achieved for its own sake."[25]

In the aftermath of *Grutter* and *Gratz*, the voters of Michigan adopted a state constitutional amendment (known as Proposal 2), prohibiting the use of race-based preferences in a wide variety of areas, including university admissions. The Supreme Court ruled on the validity of Proposal 2 in *Schuette v. Coalition to Defend Affirmative Action* (2014) (Kennedy). Justice Kennedy wrote a plurality opinion, delivering the judgment of the Court to uphold Proposal 2, but there was no majority opinion (in addition to Kennedy's plurality opinion, there were three concurrences in part, one dissent, and one Justice not taking part). The Kennedy opinion specifically held that the case "is not about the constitutionality, or the merits, of race-conscious admissions policies in higher education."[26] Instead, the opinion examined whether there was an equal protection violation by virtue of the *method* by which Michigan excluded race-based determinations from policies in state actions (including university admissions). He concluded: "There is no authority in the Constitution of the United States or in this Court's precedents for the Judiciary to set aside Michigan laws that commit this policy determination to the voters. Deliberative debate on sensitive issues such as racial preferences all too often may shade into rancor. But that does not justify removing certain court-determined issues from the voters' reach. Democracy does not presume that some subjects are either too divisive or too profound for public debate."[27] This case definitely was a scorecard opinion where few agreed on any single rationale or approach for resolving

---

[25] Parents Involved in Cmty. Sch. v. Seattle Sch. Dist. No. 1, 551 U.S. 701, 729-30 (2007).

[26] Schuette v. Coal. to Defend Affirmative Action, Integration & Immigrant Rts. & Fight for Equal. By Any Means Necessary (BAMN), 572 U.S. 291, 300 (2014).

[27] Id. at 314 (citations omitted).

the case, but a majority ultimately upheld Proposal 2 and the ban on certain affirmative action policies in the Michigan Constitution.

The next case to consider in this area is *Fisher v. University of Texas* (2016) (Kennedy), applying this line of case law, through *Grutter* and *Gratz*. *Fisher* involved a challenge to the Texas "Top Ten Percent Law," which "guarantees college admission to students who graduate from a Texas high school in the top 10 percent of their class. Those students may choose to attend any of the public universities in the State."[28] (This was actually the second time the Court ruled on this matter, as the issue went back and forth between the lower courts.) That method filled about 75% of the freshman class, so as a practical matter, students would have to finish in the top seven or eight percent of their class to be guaranteed admission. To fill out the remaining 25% of the class, the University used a score that employed numerous factors; race was considered, but not as a specific plus-factor: "although admissions officers can consider race as a positive feature of a minority student's application, there is no dispute that race is but a 'factor of a factor of a factor' in the holistic review calculus."[29] A high school student who didn't have the grades to get in under the automatic entry was considered for the remainder of the class and denied admission, and she challenged the law as unconstitutional. The Court confirmed prior case law (particularly *Grutter* and *Gratz*), holding that a university may employ a race-conscious admissions process "as a means of obtaining 'the educational benefits that flow from student body diversity.' "[30] The Court applied strict scrutiny and found that the Texas plan was constitutional. While the majority held that strict scrutiny must apply, it also said that "considerable deference is owed to" the University of Texas in

---

[28] Fisher v. Univ. of Texas At Austin, 579 U.S. 365, 372 (2016).

[29] Id. at 375.

[30] Id. at 381.

carrying out its Top Ten Percent admissions policy.[31] In dissent, Justice Alito argued that UT failed to satisfy strict scrutiny, and that the majority's deference was inconsistent with the meaning of strict scrutiny (especially in light of its first *Fisher* opinion): "What is at stake is whether university administrators may justify systematic racial discrimination simply by asserting that such discrimination is necessary to achieve 'the educational benefits of diversity,' without explaining—much less proving—why the discrimination is needed or how the discriminatory plan is well crafted to achieve its objectives."[32]

This brings our discussion to the most recent race-based admissions case, *Students for Fair Admissions v. Harvard College* (2023) (Roberts) ("*SFFA*"). *SFFA* involved the admissions processes of both Harvard College and the University of North Carolina. The Court focused heavily on Harvard's three-tiered admissions process. In the first step of the process, students might be rated individually by admissions officers as well as subcommittees assigned by geographical areas. After this step was completed, the entirety of Harvard's admissions committee would meet and vote on which applicants could be accepted based on the recommendations from the prior step; students who received at least a majority of votes from the committee would move on to the last stage. The final stage of this process would see one final cut, in which the admissions committee would only consider four aspects of the applicant: "legacy status, recruited athlete status, financial aid eligibility, and race."[33] Although a primary aspect of the final stage, Harvard allowed race to be considered in all three stages, with the admissions committee being made aware of both the racial breakdown of the entire applicant pool as well as the racial

---

[31] Id. at 388.

[32] Id. at 437 (Alito, dissenting).

[33] Students for Fair Admissions, Inc. v. President & Fellows of Harvard Coll., 600 U.S. 181, 195 (2023).

breakdown of the individual applicants who survived the second stage.

Just as it did in *Fisher*, the Court applied strict scrutiny to the admissions programs, but the *SFFA* Court differed in the amount of deference given to the universities. The Court described the review level as "daunting," very heavily reviewing both the universities' interest and the means used to achieve this interest. Chief Justice Roberts wrote that the universities must "operate their race-based admissions programs in a manner that is 'sufficiently measurable to permit judicial [review]' under the rubric of strict scrutiny. 'Classifying and assigning' students based on their race 'requires more than . . . an amorphous end to justify it.' "[34] The Court demanded that the universities not only have compelling goals but that they must be "sufficiently measurable" so that a court may review it. Harvard identified the following goals: "(1) 'training future leaders in the public and private sectors'; (2) preparing graduates to 'adapt to an increasingly pluralistic society'; (3) 'better educating its students through diversity'; and (4) 'producing new knowledge stemming from diverse outlooks.' "[35] Roberts did not believe that these goals were constitutionally-permissible, writing: "Although these are commendable goals, they are not sufficiently coherent for purposes of strict scrutiny. At the outset, it is unclear how courts are supposed to measure any of these goals. How is a court to know whether leaders have been adequately 'train[ed]'; whether the exchange of ideas is 'robust'; or whether 'new knowledge' is being developed? Even if these goals could somehow be measured, moreover, how is a court to know when they have been reached, and when the perilous remedy of racial preferences may cease? There is no particular point at which there exists sufficient 'innovation and problem-solving,' or students who

---

[34] Id. at 214 (citations omitted) (alterations in original).

[35] Id.

are appropriately 'engaged and productive.' Finally, the question in this context is not one of no diversity or of some: it is a question of degree. How many fewer leaders Harvard would create without racial preferences, or how much poorer the education at Harvard would be, are inquiries no court could resolve."[36]

Not only did Roberts take issue with the stated goals of the use of race in admissions, but he also found that the use of race was not proven to be necessary to meet the goals offered. Specifically, Roberts found that the racial classifications used were "imprecise in many ways."[37] Both "universities measure[d] the racial composition of their classes using the following categories: (1) Asian; (2) Native Hawaiian or Pacific Islander; (3) Hispanic; (4) White; (5) African-American; and (6) Native American."[38] Roberts found that the classifications used were superficial, writing: "Some of them are plainly overbroad: by grouping together all Asian students, for instance, respondents are apparently uninterested in whether South Asian or East Asian students are adequately represented, so long as there is enough of one to compensate for a lack of the other. Meanwhile other racial categories, such as 'Hispanic,' are arbitrary or undefined. And still other categories are underinclusive."[39] The majority found that there was not a meaningful connection between the goal of racial diversity and the use of these categories. Specifically, the opinion held that "the use of these opaque racial categories undermines, instead of promotes, respondents' goals. By focusing on underrepresentation, respondents would apparently prefer a class with 15% of students from Mexico over a class with 10% of students from several Latin American countries, simply because the former contains more

---

[36] Id. at 214-15 (citations omitted) (alteration in original).

[37] Id. at 216.

[38] Id.

[39] Id. (citations omitted) (alterations in original).

Hispanic students than the latter."[40] Since the admissions programs failed to meet both aspects of strict scrutiny, the Court ruled that the programs violated equal protection. Interestingly, the Chief Justice left open room for consideration of race as follows: "as all parties agree, nothing in this opinion should be construed as prohibiting universities from considering an applicant's discussion of how race affected his or her life, be it through discrimination, inspiration, or otherwise."

What's the takeaway? The *SFFA* court further developed the application of strict scrutiny in the context of race-based admissions. Following Justice Alito's dissent in *Fisher*, the Court greatly limited the deference given to universities seeking to include race in their admissions processes. In the 70+ years since *Brown* was decided, we have seen a constant pattern of reducing the deference given to educational institutions seeking to increase diversity in their student bodies.

Why do we read these last several cases? These opinions help us confront and discuss a central question about the ongoing meaning of *Brown* and the constitutional promise of equality. In his *SFFA* majority opinion, Chief Justice Roberts wrote: Eliminating racial discrimination means eliminating all of it. And the Equal Protection Clause, we have accordingly held, applies "without regard to any differences of race, of color, or of nationality"—it is "universal in [its] application." For "[t]he guarantee of equal protection cannot mean one thing when applied to one individual and something else when applied to a person of another color. If both are not accorded the same protection, then it is not equal." Roberts closed his *Parents Involved* opinion with another admonition: "Before *Brown*, schoolchildren were told where they could and could not go to school based on the color of their skin. The school districts in these cases have not carried the heavy burden

---

40 Id.

of demonstrating that we should allow this once again—even for very different reasons. For schools that never segregated on the basis of race, such as Seattle, or that have removed the vestiges of past segregation, such as Jefferson County, the way 'to achieve a system of determining admission to the public schools on a nonracial basis' is to stop assigning students on a racial basis. The way to stop discrimination on the basis of race is to stop discriminating on the basis of race."[41] In his concurrence, Justice Kennedy argued for greater flexibility when it comes to race-based programs, finding the majority approach perhaps too simplistic. He wrote, "This Nation has a moral and ethical obligation to fulfill its historic commitment to creating an integrated society that ensures equal opportunity for all of its children."[42] Justice Stevens dissented strongly, arguing that the majority failed to acknowledge that blacks were the ones denied opportunity in the cases that brought us to *Brown*. Invoking that landmark decision in this way, he argued, distorted the meaning. Justice Breyer dissented to argue that the opinion undermines 50 years of schools' attempts to integrate under *Brown* and that it opens up more litigation. Justice Sotomayor's lengthy dissent in *Schuette* also engaged in a broad discourse on the meaning and importance of race in America and the constitutional promise of the Fourteenth Amendment, offering yet another compelling voice to the debate. She wrote: "In my colleagues' view, examining the racial impact of legislation only perpetuates racial discrimination. This refusal to accept the stark reality that race matters is regrettable. The way to stop discrimination on the basis of race is to speak openly and candidly on the subject of race, and to apply the Constitution with eyes open to the unfortunate effects of centuries of racial discrimination. As members of the judiciary tasked with intervening to carry out the guarantee of equal protection, we ought not sit back and wish away,

---

[41] Parents Involved, 551 U.S. at 747-48 (2007) (citations omitted).

[42] Id. at 797 (Kennedy, concurring).

rather than confront, the racial inequality that exists in our society."[43] Justice Alito's *Fisher* dissent, as noted before, further raises questions of how to define the compelling governmental interest in diversity in education, and what deference is appropriate to offer educational institutions.

Those clear fault lines are at the center of a grand legal-philosophical debate within the judicial branch, among legislators, and with academics today. With its changed composition, the Court is less likely than ever to defer to educational institutions' plans and programs to achieve diversity in their student body. There is more clearly an "answer" to questions of what methods may be used to promote diversity, but there remains a very significant discussion over the meaning of the Equal Protection Clause and *Brown* which you should understand as you study these materials in Con Law.

Overview

We have seen a lot of material, and here are a few points to highlight for the big picture:

- Race-conscious government programs must survive strict scrutiny Equal Protection Clause analysis;
- The race of the parties involved does not matter—black, white, or other;
- Invidious v. benign programs—there is no difference, constitutionally speaking;
- Broad goals of educational diversity are not absolutely unacceptable—but they appear to be disfavored;
- Race may be a factor but may not be the factor;

[43] Schuette, 572 U.S. at 381 (Sotomayor, dissenting).

- Many Justices continue to disagree over what approach is the best fit, both functionally and constitutionally.

C. Intermediate Scrutiny and Gender Cases

The Court has reviewed gender classifications using intermediate scrutiny. One of the first cases to deal with a gender-based classification was *Bradwell v. Illinois* (1872) (Miller), upholding a law that prohibited women from becoming licensed to practice law. One concurrence observed that it is "[t]he paramount destiny and mission of women to fulfill the noble and benign offices of wife and mother [which] is the law of the Creator."[44] The Court believed that it was not a woman's role to become a lawyer. With women now making up more than half of the population entering law school, it seems that the attitude from the *Bradwell* decision has not prevailed. The analytical point here is that there was no searching inquiry about gender-based classifications for nearly a century. *Reed v. Reed* (1971) (Burger) was the first time the Court invalidated a gender-based classification, and it used a rational basis review. In *Frontiero v. Richardson* (1973) (Brennan), there was an argument that there should be heightened scrutiny for gender classifications but still, there was no clear majority for using heightened scrutiny to review gender-based classifications.

The first time the Court employed heightened scrutiny in a case involving gender was in the 1976 decision in *Craig v. Boren* (Brennan). An Oklahoma law allowed women to buy 3.2% alcohol "near beer" at age 18; men could not do so until age 21. The law purported to advance safety objectives related to teenage males' propensity for drinking and driving. The Court declared the law unconstitutional, using intermediate scrutiny to analyze gender

---

[44] Bradwell v. People of State of Illinois, 83 U.S. 130, 141 (1872) (Bradley, concurring).

classifications. "To withstand constitutional challenge, previous cases establish that classifications by gender must serve *important governmental objectives* and must be *substantially related* to achievement of those objectives."[45] While traffic safety was seen as an important objective, the statistics presented *did not establish the proper fit*—it was "tenuous." But the Court did use some sort of heightened scrutiny more searching than rational basis review.

The definitive case is *United States v. Virginia* (1996) (Ginsburg), a challenge to the all-male Virginia Military Institute (VMI), which had been in existence since 1839. VMI, an elite college designed to produce citizen-soldiers, employed an "adversative" approach. It was what you might think of as stereotypical boot camp-type training, designed to breed loyalty, mental and physical discipline, etc. The school was very successful and prestigious—and all-male. Women seeking admission sued and won in the lower federal courts. As a result, Virginia created the Virginia Women's Institute for Leadership at Mary Baldwin College, but that program did not use the same training methods, inhabited different facilities, did not employ a military approach, and did not connect its students with the extensive VMI alumni network.

This new arrangement ultimately was challenged in the Supreme Court, and the Court held the exclusion of women by VMI to be unconstitutional. The key analytical point was that the majority employed intermediate scrutiny, requiring an "exceedingly persuasive justification," with the burden on the government to prove an important objective and substantial relation.[46] The government's justification could "not rely on overbroad generalizations about the different talents, capacities, or preferences of males and females."[47] And in carrying through this

---

[45] Craig v. Boren, 429 U.S. 190, 197 (1976) (emphasis added).

[46] United States v. Virginia, 518 U.S. 515, 531 (1996).

[47] Id. at 533.

analysis, the Court held that VMI's exclusion of women was unconstitutional because it was based entirely on gender stereotypes.

Putting it all in context, the Court reviewed the history of separate educational facilities in this country, at one point emphasizing that the successful integration of the federal military academies undercut the fundamental arguments made by VMI. The two principle reasons for rejecting the VMI/VWIL plan were: (1) it was not a valid effort to diversify educational opportunity, as it simply provided unique opportunities to Virginia's sons, but not to its daughters; and (2) the Court was not persuaded that the need to preserve the adversative method for men sufficed to maintain VMI as an all-male institution. Some men might not like it, and some women might or might not like it. But the government could not base its decision on a broad-based stereotype.

What's the takeaway? Intermediate scrutiny must be employed when reviewing gender-based classifications under the Equal Protection Clause. That requires the government to meet an exceedingly persuasive burden of proof that the means chosen bear a substantial relation to an important government objective. In this case, Virginia failed to meet its burden and VMI had to open its doors to women.

There's also a question of how to analyze gender-based classifications under the Equal Protection Clause—*why heightened scrutiny*? The textual foundation is in the Fourteenth Amendment, but the text does not explicitly mention gender. When you look at the ratification debates over the Fifteenth Amendment, you see that Congress rejected gender equality arguments and the idea that women should be also be extended the right to vote. Ultimately, the Nineteenth Amendment took care of that, but it said no more in terms of equality for women. So, what's the point? What do we do? The courts have tried to analogize between gender and race.

Because gender and race are *similar* in some relevant ways, yet dissimilar in others, the Court has settled with intermediate scrutiny—more than rational basis, but not as exacting as strict scrutiny.

Why do we read and discuss the VMI case? This case is important for firmly establishing heightened scrutiny for gender-based classifications, but it also raises questions about just what that scrutiny is. The "exceedingly persuasive justification" language suggests something more than what has traditionally been considered intermediate scrutiny. This is often referred to as intermediate-plus, or with "bite". And all of that calls into question the conventional wisdom that there are three set tiers of scrutiny.

Additionally, there is a core debate, as expressed in Justice Scalia's dissent about the importance and meaning of Equal Protection, plus the Court's role as a guardian of individual rights. He argues that this was inappropriate judicial activism and that the majority instead should have employed rational basis review. "Today, . . . change is forced upon Virginia, and reversion to single-sex education is prohibited nationwide, not by democratic processes but by order of this Court. . . . The enemies of single-sex education have won; by persuading only seven Justices. . . that their view of the world is enshrined in the Constitution, they have effectively imposed that view on all 50 States."[48] In other words, Justice Scalia believes that if the people of Virginia, acting through their legislature, want to establish single-sex educational facilities, then they may do so. Let the people decide through democratic processes. But the majority frames the case as being about individual rights, as protected by the Equal Protection Clause. And the Court ultimately is the guarantor of those rights; the people—through a majority vote, an executive act or otherwise—cannot take

[48] Id. at 570, 597 (1996) (Scalia, dissenting).

away what the Constitution promises to us all through a simple majority.

D. Rational Basis

The lowest level of scrutiny, rational basis review, applies at a minimum to all classifications under Equal Protection analysis. One example you will see can be found in the context of **disability**, in *City of Cleburne v. Cleburne Living Center* (1985) (White). That case involved a challenge to a city ordinance requiring a special permit for operation of a group home for the mentally disabled. Lower court findings established that the city denied a permit for the group home for some of the following reasons:

1. A negative attitude among a majority of local property owners;
2. A junior high school across the street and fear of the residents being teased by the school children; and
3. The home's location on a flood plain.

The law classified on the basis of mental ability, leaving the question of what level of scrutiny to apply. The starting point was the general rule "that legislation is presumed to be valid and will be sustained if the classification drawn by the statute is *rationally related* to a legitimate state interest."[49] When race, alienage, or national origin form the basis of the classification, heightened scrutiny is required, because such factors are so rarely relevant to achievement of a legitimate state interest. Likewise, gender classifications call for "somewhat heightened scrutiny." Here, the appropriate level of scrutiny was the minimal *rational relation test*

[49] City of Cleburne, Tex. v. Cleburne Living Ctr., 473 U.S. 432, 440 (1985) (emphasis added).

"requir[ing] only a rational means to serve a legitimate end."[50] This law failed rational basis scrutiny because:

1. The property owners' attitudes were insufficient as a basis for treating the home differently;
2. Special needs students attended the junior high school; and
3. The flood plain justification did not apply to the permitting process for homes for the elderly, for example, so it was rejected.

"The short of it is that requiring the permit in this case appears to us to rest on an irrational prejudice against the mentally retarded."[51] This specific government action of grouping people failed such scrutiny. Rational basis can always apply in any situation, and specifically it has been applied in cases to analyze allegations of the denial of equal protection under law on the basis of disability, age and poverty. Other categorizations, if not a suspect or "quasi-suspect" classification, would also face such minimal scrutiny.

E. Sexual Orientation

With those classifications and tiers of scrutiny set in the case law, in recent years the Court has spoken to one more question: classifications on the basis of **sexual orientation**. As Justice Brennan argued in 1985, "homosexuals constitute a significant and insular minority of this country's population. Because of the immediate and severe opprobrium often manifested against homosexuals once so identified publicly, members of this group are particularly powerless to pursue their rights openly in the political arena. Moreover, homosexuals have historically been the object of pernicious and sustained hostility, and it is fair to say that

50 Id. at 442.

51 Id. at 450.

discrimination against homosexuals is 'likely . . . to reflect deep-seated prejudice rather than . . . rationality.' "[52] To the extent that sexual orientation is an immutable characteristic, that would argue further for heightened scrutiny. But it is also unlike race and gender, as one's race or gender can be immediately apparent, without stereotyping or assumption. While sexual orientation is part of who one is, it can also be manifested through actions—conduct, as opposed to status. Our societal understanding is evolving, and recent cases give a developing legal framework for Equal Protection analysis.

First, one seminal case is *Romer v. Evans* (1996) (Kennedy), which involved a challenge to Colorado's "Amendment 2." In response to the inclusion of homosexuality as a class of persons statutorily protected from discrimination in various state and local laws, Colorado voters passed Amendment 2. This prohibited the government from enacting, adopting, or enforcing any statute that provided any special advantages or any protected status for homosexuals. It effectively barred any state law claim of discrimination or protected status on the basis of homosexuality. In challenging Amendment 2, several theories were presented to the Court, including urging the Justices to grant sexual orientation *suspect classification* mandating (some level of) *heightened scrutiny* for classifications based on sexual orientation. The Court did not do so, but it did strike Amendment 2 in part because it was a rare example of a *literal denial of equal protection* of the law. While a state is under no obligation to provide anyone with protection from discrimination, it cannot constitutionally excise any one group from protection. "Amendment 2. . . is at once too narrow and too broad. It identifies persons by a single trait and then denies them protection across the board. The resulting disqualification of

[52] Rowland v. Mad River Local Sch. Dist., Montgomery County, Ohio, 470 U.S. 1009, 1014 (1985) (footnotes omitted) (alterations in original).

a class of persons from the right to seek specific protection from the law is unprecedented in our jurisprudence. . . . It is not within our constitutional tradition to enact laws of this sort."[53]

In addition, the Court held that the law rested solely on *irrational prejudice against homosexuals* and thus denied equal protection, under rationality review. "Amendment 2, . . . in making a general announcement that gays and lesbians shall not have any particular protections from the law, inflicts on them immediate, continuing, and real injuries that outrun and belie any legitimate justifications that may be claimed for it."[54] Lacking any rational relation to a legitimate governmental purpose, the law could not survive even minimal constitutional scrutiny. The Court summed it up as follows: "It is a status-based enactment divorced from any factual context from which we could discern a relationship to legitimate state interests; it is a classification of persons undertaken for its own sake, something the Equal Protection Clause does not permit."[55] The Court saw this as an irrational attempt to single-out homosexuals for lesser legal status, contrary to the constitutional mandate of equal protection under law.

What's the takeaway? This was the first case to extend the reach of the Equal Protection Clause to gays and lesbians. However, the Court did not rule that discrimination based on sexual orientation warrants heightened scrutiny; only rational basis review was employed. But even under this minimal standard, Colorado's Amendment 2 could not stand.

Why do we read and discuss *Romer v. Evans*? First, this case signals a major shift in the Court's approach towards gays and lesbians, and I encourage you to read this and compare it with what happened in *Bowers v. Hardwick* (1986) (White) and *Lawrence v.*

---

[53] Romer v. Evans, 517 U.S. 620, 633 (1996).

[54] Id. at 635.

[55] Id.

Texas (2003) (Kennedy) (see Chapter 9). The two more recent cases (in 1996 and 2003) both established greater protections against regulations that treated homosexuals differently. When I started law school in 1989, *Bowers* had just been decided on a 5-4 vote, and homosexual sodomy was outlawed without any Due Process concerns, much less Equal Protection. But new thinking has prevailed on the Court in both areas, more broadly rejecting attempts to treat homosexuals as a class apart. Justice Scalia's harsh dissent in *Romer* argued that the Court had no role in this field: "Since the Constitution of the United States says nothing about this subject, it is left to be resolved by normal democratic means."[56] So, was Scalia simply disagreeing with a political result he does not like, or was Kennedy simply stepping in to impose values in a political battle? As Scalia maintained, "Of course it is our moral heritage that one should not hate any human being or class of human beings. But I had thought that one could consider certain conduct reprehensible—murder, for example or polygamy, or cruelty to animals—and could exhibit even 'animus' toward such conduct. Surely that is the only sort of 'animus' at issue here[.]"[57] The reply by Kennedy's majority opinion was that we are protecting individual rights here, and no majority can take away the equality protected by the Constitution. So in the end, according to the majority this is *exactly* the place for the Court: interpreting a constitutional mandate and protecting individual rights.

Further, do you think *Bowers* should have controlled the Court's opinion in *Romer*? *Bowers* denied a Due Process attack to an anti-sodomy law, rejecting any right of privacy exclusively to homosexual sodomy. So, ask yourself, is this an extension of that case? (And remember that *Bowers* was good law at the time *Romer* was decided, so *Lawrence* didn't apply.) The starting point is that

---

[56] Id. at 636 (Scalia, dissenting).

[57] Id. at 644 (Scalia, dissenting).

Bowers was a Due Process case and that the Equal Protection Clause is a separate matter. Due Process Clause privacy concerns are different than Equal Protection Clause concerns—the former concerns privacy and the latter cares about how people are classified on the basis of some characteristic. Furthermore, not all homosexuals engage in homosexual sodomy, and the inference of conduct from status is impermissible. In the end, it is essential to recognize that the Court has now stricken laws that treat homosexuals differently on the basis of sexual orientation; the opprobrium that Justice Scalia mentions in his dissent has no foundation in the Constitution.

So the next question to consider is **same-sex marriage**, as discussed in *U.S. v. Windsor* (2013) (Kennedy), *Hollingsworth v. Perry* (2013) (Roberts), and *Obergefell v. Hodges* (2015) (Kennedy). In *Windsor* the Court explored the application of the federal Defense of Marriage Act (DOMA), which in relevant part excluded a same-sex partner from the definition of "spouse" as that term is used in countless federal statutes. In this case, it had a specific negative federal tax impact on the surviving spouse of a same-sex marriage that had been performed and recognized in New York state. Writing for the Court, Justice Kennedy observed that states have long had exclusive power over marriage and that the federal government historically has deferred to state-law policy decisions with respect to domestic relations. DOMA departed from the tradition of reliance on state law to define marriage. But he found that to be inconsistent with the Constitution's guarantee of equality, writing that a bare congressional desire to harm a group cannot justify disparate treatment of that group. As the law was designed to make same-sex marriages essentially second-class marriages, the Court wrote, "DOMA writes inequality into the entire United States Code,"[58] and held DOMA unconstitutional. Furthermore, Kennedy wrote that

[58] U.S. v. Windsor, 570 U.S. 744, 771 (2013).

DOMA demeans same-sex couples, whose sexual and moral choices are protected by the Constitution, and it is unconstitutional as a deprivation of liberty under the Fifth Amendment's Due Process Clause.

While many saw *Windsor* as a constitutional victory for same-sex marriage, on that same day the Court announced its decision in *Hollingsworth v. Perry* (2013) (Roberts), ruling on a same-sex marriage case without resolving the key underlying due process and equal protection issues.

In short, the following occurred: after a challenge in state court, the California Supreme Court had ruled to strike down its state statutes limiting marriage to opposite-sex individuals. In response, the electorate voted for Proposition 8, which effectively reinstated the ban on same-sex marriage. The U.S. District Court in San Francisco, with extensive findings of fact, then overturned Proposition 8 on both equal protection and due process grounds, a ruling which was affirmed by the Ninth Circuit U.S. Court of Appeals. When *Hollingsworth* made it to the Supreme Court, with *Windsor* also on the docket, many saw the two cases as a chance for clarity from the Court on all constitutional questions related to same-sex marriage. But the Court ruled on unrelated procedural grounds, holding that petitioners didn't have standing to appeal to the Ninth Circuit's decision, so the District Court ruling stood. As the decision was essentially procedural in nature, the *Hollingsworth* Court did not address the underlying merits regarding same-sex marriage.

In sum, the *Windsor* Court left some ambiguity as to its sources and scope, as it addressed both equality and due process issues. *Hollingsworth* declined to address the core substantive issues we are discussing here. So questions remained. *Obergefell* addressed those questions with greater certainty.

Obergefell came in the context of significant movement among the states approving same-sex marriage, by statue, court ruling, or voter initiative. This case specifically presented the legal questions of whether the Fourteenth Amendment requires states to license same-sex marriages, and whether it requires states to recognize same-sex marriages licensed and performed in other states. The Court held in the affirmative, thus enshrining same-sex marriage within protected constitutional space. Noting that historically, marriage was seen and codified as only between a man and a woman, the Court also acknowledged the changes in law and society. Comparing changes in the legal status of women, Kennedy saw similar change with respect to gay rights. Kennedy also opined, "sexual orientation is both a normal expression of human sexuality and immutable."[59] In a similar vein, the Court observed the development of its own jurisprudence in the area of gay rights.

Getting to the specific question presented, the Court looked at the long line of case law protecting the right of marriage (including *Loving*, discussed earlier in this chapter). The Court then denoted four major concepts that support the holding that the Fourteenth Amendment requires a state to license same-sex marriages and acknowledge same-sex marriages from other states: (1) the right to choose whether and whom to marry is "inherent in the concept of individual autonomy;"[60] (2) the right to marry serves relationships that are equal in importance to all who enter them; (3) marriage protects children and families, "draw[ing] meaning from related rights of childrearing, procreation, and education;"[61] and (4) marriage is the very "keystone of our social order" and the foundation of the family unit.[62]

After reviewing those principles, the Court concluded that same-sex marriage is protected under the U.S. Constitution. "The limitation of marriage to opposite-sex couples may long have

---

59 Obergefell v. Hodges, 576 U.S. 644, 661 (2015).

60 Id. at 665.

61 Id. at 667.

62 Id. at 669.

seemed natural and just, but its inconsistency with the central meaning of the fundamental right to marry is now manifest. With that knowledge must come the recognition that laws excluding same-sex couples from the marriage right impose stigma and injury of the kind prohibited by our basic charter."[63] The Court further held: "It is now clear that the challenged laws burden the liberty of same-sex couples, and it must be further acknowledged that they abridge central precepts of equality."[64] Same-sex marriage is legal in all states. Importantly, Justice Kennedy acknowledged that this is a matter that has been, and at the time was being, debated in the various state legislatures. But, as a matter of constitutional law, he emphasized that "[t]he dynamic of our constitutional system is that individuals need not await legislative action before asserting a fundamental right."[65] The purpose of the courts is to enforce legal and constitutional rights.

Chief Justice Roberts dissented, arguing that the majority was inappropriately making a policy decision: "But this Court is not a legislature. Whether same-sex marriage is a good idea should be of no concern to us. Under the Constitution, judges have power to say what the law is, not what it should be."[66] Similarly, Justices Scalia, Thomas and Alito joined and wrote dissents, arguing against what they saw as judicial "hubris" (Scalia)[67] and "abuse of [the Court's] authority" (Alito),[68] and a threat to democracy and democratic processes.

What's the takeaway? The Court held: "same-sex couples may exercise the fundamental right to marry."[69] This applies to all

---

[63] Id. at 670-71.
[64] Id. at 675.
[65] Id. at 677.
[66] Id. at 686 (Roberts, dissenting).
[67] Id. at 720 (Scalia, dissenting).
[68] Id. at 742 (Alito, dissenting).
[69] Id. at 647.

states, so that they must license same-sex couples and must recognize the validity of same-sex marriages performed in other states.

Why do we read and discuss these cases? These cases are important for the obvious reason that they declared same-sex marriage to be protected by the Constitution of the United States, but there's more. These cases go to the heart of methods of constitutional interpretation. How do we interpret the Great Document in our ever-changing world? The term *same-sex marriage* is clearly not in the text, and nobody disputes that the Framers didn't endorse the concept, but that cannot be the beginning and the end of the discussion. In seeking answers, the majority opined: "The history of marriage is one of both *continuity* and *change*. That institution—even as confined to opposite-sex relations—has *evolved* over time."[70] It is telling that Justice Kennedy used this language in his analysis, perhaps reflecting a larger view on how to approach some constitutional questions. So, the challenge to the majority is to clearly define how we decide what is a protected, unenumerated constitutional right? "The identification and protection of fundamental rights is an enduring part of the judicial duty to interpret the Constitution . . . [in a manner that] respects our history and learns from it without allowing the past alone to rule the present."[71] Justice Kennedy added, "If rights were defined by who exercised them in the past, then received practices could serve as their own continued justification and new groups could not invoke rights once denied. This Court has rejected that approach, both with respect to the right to marry and the rights of gays and lesbians."[72] The dissenters would leave this question to the people, through state government, and they decried the Court's holding. While there is a serious question of what the role of the Court is, the challenge

[70] Id. at 659 (emphasis added).

[71] Id. at 664.

[72] Id. at 671.

to the dissent is where we draw lines. An easy extension of their argument is that *Brown v. Board of Education* was wrongly decided. While I do not think the dissenters would argue that, they still leave open the question of how we address changes in 21st century society, in the context of a constitution that was written and ratified in the 18th century.

A further challenge that goes to **why we read and discuss** these cases comes with the intersection of the Due Process Clause and the Equal Protection Clause. While we are discussing this in our chapter on Equal Protection, it is clearly a decision about both clauses/fields. Justice Kennedy wrote: "The Due Process Clause and the Equal Protection Clause are connected in a profound way, though they set forth independent principles. Rights implicit in liberty and rights secured by equal protection may rest on different precepts and are not always coextensive, yet in some instances each may be instructive as to the meaning and reach of the other."[73] The previous cases addressing gay rights did not directly address this issue in such a manner, and these words from *Obergefell* provide us all with an interesting issue to consider for how we analyze the intersection of these two parts of the Constitution . . . and perhaps others.

F. Fundamental Rights

Equal Protection Clause analysis sometimes dictates heightened scrutiny, not because of a suspect classification, but rather because of an attack on a *fundamental interest*. In those cases, the Court finds that a fundamental right is so particularly or uniquely important to the nation that it deserves special protection, via strict scrutiny. We quickly look at voting, which has been held to be a fundamental right, and then to education, which has not.

---

[73] Id. at 672.

Voting Rights

There are many references to the right to vote in various constitutional amendments, including the Fifteenth (no denial based on race or previous condition of servitude); the Nineteenth (extending the right to women); the Twenty-fourth (prohibiting poll taxes); and the Twenty-sixth (granting 18-year-olds the right to vote). In case law, the Court has often expressed and affirmed that the right to vote is fundamental and deserving of protection pursuant to the Equal Protection Clause. It is fundamental at least in part as a necessary ingredient of America's representative government, and restrictions on the basic right to vote must be subject to strict scrutiny.

Early cases like *Harper v. Virginia State Board of Elections* (1966) (Douglas) held the poll tax unconstitutional (before the Twenty-fourth Amendment), employing Equal Protection analysis. Just as the Twenty-fourth Amendment had prohibited poll taxes in federal elections in 1964, this case extended that rule to state elections. In *Kramer v. Union Free School District No. 15* (1969) (Warren), the Court held that, under an Equal Protection analysis, property ownership qualifications fail strict scrutiny.

The major cases in this area that you will study in Con Law deal with vote dilution, reapportionment, and gerrymandering. Prior to the 1960's, many state legislatures were malapportioned—one district would be much more populous than another for the same legislative body. Malapportioned districts often resulted because of population shifts—as urban areas grew, districts were not redrawn, causing cities to be under-represented. (Those legislators who benefitted didn't want change, so the political process was non-responsive.) At first, cases concerning malapportioned districts were held to present non-justiciable political questions, but *Baker v. Carr* (see Chapter 3) opened the door. The Court began to articulate a constitutional basis: the one-person, one-vote concept.

For any one legislative body, all districts must have approximately the same number of people. *Why was this a constitutional problem?* The effect of lodging greater power in some people's votes than in others meant unequal political power. The Court held that the Equal Protection Clause required that all districts be equipopulous—anything else impermissibly diluted the voting power of those who resided in more populous districts.

The key case you will read is *Reynolds v. Sims* (1964) (Warren). The Alabama legislature had a 35 member Senate, elected from 35 districts ranging in population from 15,417 to 634,864 people; its 100 member House of Representatives had districts with populations ranging from 31,175 to 634,864. The districts had been drawn based on the 1900 census. In analyzing these districts, Chief Justice Warren started with a conclusion that the Constitution stands for the proposition of equal representation for equal numbers of people. He observed that geographical area made no sense in drawing districts—only population was a permissible basis. "Legislators represent people, not trees or acres. Legislators are elected by voters, not farms or cities or economic interests. As long as ours is a representative form of government, and our legislatures are those instruments of government elected directly by and directly representative of the people, the right to elect legislatures in a free and unimpaired fashion is a bedrock of our political system."[74] Malapportionment, the Court explained, meant vote dilution—voters in the more populous districts have proportionately less influence than those in the small population districts. "If a State should provide that the votes of citizens in one part of the State should be given two times, or five times, or 10 times the weight of votes of citizens in another part of the State, it could hardly be contended that the right to vote of those residing in the disfavored

[74] Reynolds v. Sims, 377 U.S. 533, 562 (1964).

areas had not been effectively diluted."[75] The Court held that representative government needs, and even demands, that the majority can express its political will in electing their representatives. The Constitution will prevent against other abuses by the majority. The Court concluded that both houses of a state legislature must be apportioned on a population basis.

What's the takeaway? One-person, one-vote is constitutionally required, and legislative districts in state governments must be equipopulous. The Court did not require mathematical certainty but rather a good-faith effort to achieve mathematical equality. (At the time, it was harder to achieve, but with today's computer programs and voter data availability even greater precision is achievable and expected.)

Why do we read and discuss these materials? The one-person, one-vote cases were somewhat controversial at the time, but now they are more widely accepted. The underlying issue is whether the Court was *engaging in (impermissible) political action*—or—was it acting *to perfect the political process, to protect individual rights, and to reinforce democracy*. Districts were unlikely to change without judicial intervention because the officeholders were likely to lose their seats and/or power and thus unwilling to act, so the Court stepped in. Still, where, in the text or the Framers' intent, is this specific one-person, one-vote rule? In any event, the Court held here that it was protecting individual rights; although acting in a political situation, the matter was not a political question but rather a matter of protecting individual rights.

Education

Unlike voting, education has *not* been held to be a fundamental right guaranteed by the U.S. Constitution. *San Antonio Independent School District v. Rodriguez* (1973) (Powell) articulated that rule.

---

[75] Id.

The Texas system of public financing schools via local property taxes had the impact that children in poorer areas had less money spent on their schools, while those in wealthier areas had more spent on their schools. Families who brought suit alleged an unconstitutional deprivation visited upon children attending the arguably inferior, less well-funded schools. The school funding system meant that poor areas had to tax at a high rate but still had little to spend on education. In contrast, wealthier areas could tax at a low rate and still have much greater resources to devote to education. As an example, one poor district spent $356 per pupil as compared to $594 in a wealthier district. The plaintiffs challenged the Texas school funding system on two grounds, arguing:

1. It violated the Equal Protection Clause because it was impermissible *wealth discrimination*; and
2. It denied plaintiffs' *fundamental right to education* implicit in the Equal Protection Clause.

First, the Court held that *poverty is not a suspect classification* and that rational basis review was appropriate. Second, the Court confronted the question of whether education is a fundamental right, holding that it is not. "[T]he key to discovering whether education is 'fundamental' is not to be found in comparisons of the relative societal significance of education as opposed to subsistence or housing. . . . Rather, the answer lies in assessing whether there is a right to education explicitly or implicitly guaranteed by the Constitution."[76] Reading the text of the Constitution, there is no explicit mention, and reading into the history, the Court found that the claimed right to education was not implicit either. The Texas system survived rational basis review.

What's the takeaway? There is no fundamental right to education in the U.S. Constitution.

---

[76] San Antonio Indep. Sch. Dist. v. Rodriguez, 411 U.S. 1, 33 (1973).

Why do we read this case? It illustrates the basic tension between reading the Constitution's text and its guarantees *broadly* and *narrowly*. The Constitution must mean more than just the explicit words in the text—it is a *constitution* we are expounding. So we cannot resolve all questions of constitutional interpretation by simply asking if the express words are present. But even so, how do we define the beginning and end of that inquiry? However we answer that question, in this case the Court finds no fundamental federal constitutional right to education.

The Court's refusal to hold education to be a fundamental interest is consistent with the belief that there is no constitutional requirement that the government provide particular benefits or services like education. But there is an additional tension to note here. In *Brown*, Chief Justice Warren wrote: "education is perhaps the most important function of state and local governments. Compulsory school attendance laws and the great expenditures for education both demonstrate our recognition of the importance of education to our democratic society. It is required in the performance of our most basic public responsibilities[.] . . . It is the very foundation of good citizenship. . . . In these days, it is doubtful that any child may reasonably be expected to succeed in life if he is denied the opportunity of an education."[77] So when we look at *San Antonio v. Rodriguez*, it may seem hard to reconcile that decision with the outlook from *Brown*. But even *Brown* emphasizes the state and local role in education as paramount. That, plus with the rule that we have just read, note that many states have, explicitly and through judicial decisions, found a guarantee to equal education through their own constitutions. And once a state decides to provide an education to its children, as every state has, the provision of such education must be consistent with other federally

---

[77] Brown v. Bd. of Ed. of Topeka, Shawnee County, Kan., 347 U.S. 483, 493 (1954).

guaranteed constitutional rights, including Equal Protection. As the Court further held in *Plyler v. Doe* (1982) (Brennan), "Public education is not a 'right' granted to individuals by the Constitution. But neither is it merely some government 'benefit' indistinguishable from other forms of social welfare legislation. Both the importance of education in maintaining our basic institutions, and the lasting impact of its deprivation on the life of the child, mark the distinction. . . . In addition, education provides the basic tools by which individuals might lead economically productive lives to the benefit of us all. In sum, education has a fundamental role in maintaining the fabric of our society."[78] In the end, there is no specific federal constitutional right to education. But it is protected at the state level, and denial of that state right still can be protected by the U.S. Constitution and courts.

[78] Plyler v. Doe, 457 U.S. 202, 221 (1982) (citations omitted).

CHAPTER 12

Top Ten Exam Tips

Having finished the substance, I want to take a few more pages to talk about some ideas I have had over time that may make your life as a law student even more enjoyable. Year after year, students ask me what to do about exams. I am always happy to share my thoughts so that I can (hopefully) take even a tiny bit of stress out of one unpleasant part of law school. So, here are my top ten tips for taking law school exams. Read them, think about them, and use them as they work for you. Remember, there is no magic formula, or else everyone would get an A+!

1. **Be confident.** Success in exams all starts on the first day of the semester. Week in and week out, you need to prepare. And as each week goes by you have to keep the confidence up and the stress down. Competition with your classmates is definitely part of the stress of law school, and sometimes you'll feel pressure that you're not studying enough, writing enough, or staying up late enough. It is important to be confident in your study habits and methods. Everyone is different, and everyone studies differently. Don't be swayed or nervous because you are not comfortable studying like your other

classmates. Although law school is hard, it also can be enjoyable. But it requires work, and there are no shortcuts. (Also read the cases throughout the semester; no outline or study aid can make up for the actual cases, not even a *Short & Happy Guide*!) So be honest and figure out what *you* need to do to make it work, and do the work. Plan your work, then work your plan. And be confident in yourself.

2. **Stay engaged in class.** As much as you need to prepare before class, what you do *in class* is essential. Because law school courses are taught predominantly in the Socratic method, you can't sit back and just absorb a lecture from a professor every day. You need to be ready, and you must *engage in class*. That means speaking when called on and raising your hand when you have a good point (but don't just be a gunner; use your discretion, and don't raise your hand constantly just because some thought popped into your head). It also means listening to what your classmates say when you are *not* on the hot seat. When the professor asks a question of someone else, think about how you would answer, listen to your classmate's reply, and consider how that reply fits within your own conception of the case.

3. **Take time to do something you enjoy**. Once you get to the end of the semester and you are in reading period and exams, you need to take care of yourself. Whether it's going to the gym, going to lunch with friends, or baking cookies, find whatever it is you enjoy during exam time and *do it*. When I was in law school, I would make a calendar for each day with blocks of time: two hours to study, then an hour for a meal; another block of studying, then a block for going to the gym. Study, then TV. You get

the point—just figure the things you want to do in-between those study blocks. If you structure your day *and stick to the plan* you can get a lot of hours in for studying while still maintaining your physical and mental health in a stressful time. This kind of structure will make your study days that much more manageable.

Tips #4-10 focus on exam-taking itself: what to do in the exam room.

4. **Read carefully**. Be careful not to misread the question or miss a page of the exam. Every word, sentence, and paragraph of the test is important to your answering each of the questions to the best of your ability . . . and that includes the directions.

5. **Stay within the call of the question**. Make sure to answer what the actual question asks; don't give into the temptation to tell all you know about a given legal topic if it's not asked for by the question. A professor will ask what he or she thinks is valuable to test you on; show your professor what you know as analytically and concisely as possible. In my experience when reading and grading Con Law exams, I would have 60-80 exams, all of them very long and very similar. I wouldn't know whose exam it was, so I couldn't fill in the blanks for *you* because I remembered that you made an insightful comment in week three of the semester. You have three or four hours to show what you have learned; take advantage of that time, and do so wisely.

6. **Outline!** At the very least think about the construction of your essay answer before writing it. Because of the intense pressure of a law school exam and the short amount of time a student has to read a fact pattern and draft a written response, students often write

without thinking about how to structure their analysis. This often leads to answers that may have the right intention but are hard for professors to comprehend. The best answers are those that clearly communicate the ideas taught and studied. Outlining or thinking before writing will significantly help to achieve this goal. Just as in Tip #5, remember that you have a short period of time to present information to the professor. Clear and concise answers are very helpful.

7. **If a specific amount of time is recommended for the questions, follow that lead.** That amount represents how much time a professor thinks you should spend on a given question. It is also typically how we will weight questions (and yes this tip applies to how to divide your time if point values or percentages are given, instead of time—just do a quick calculation before you do anything else.) Going slightly over time on one particular question is not a disaster, but if so, just pull a bit of time off each other answer to make up for it. You want to avoid pouring all of your energy, effort, time, and thought into a single question—usually this happens towards the beginning of the test—at the expense of your answers on the later questions.

8. **Use the fact pattern to construct your answer.** This may sound tautological, but it's important and something that students often forget. If a professor is including an interesting fact in the prompt, it is likely because it has legal significance in the answer. Think about the reasons a particular fact is present and try to articulate in your argument what it means and why it's important.

9. Particularly in Constitutional Law, it's helpful to **think about cases (almost invariably Supreme Court**

Cases) in the historical legal context in which they took place. This is why, as you may have noticed, I have included years and opinion authors with the first reference of each case within this book. Knowing which judges offered important majority opinions, plurality opinions, concurrences, and dissents; at what time in American history; and for what policy reasons will often help frame an exam essay argument. There are connections you will see and draw upon. This is not to say that you're writing a history paper on an exam or that you are giving a civics lesson, but merely it can be helpful and instructive to a professor for framing your argument with a bit more context.

10. **Don't freak out.** At the end of the day, it's just an exam. Keep everything in perspective. There are many factors that have an impact on your success in law school and your legal career. A single exam, or a single grade, is not going to make or break your future.

CHAPTER 13

Courage

Law school is a transformative period. When I look back on it, I am amazed at how much I learned. What I understand with hindsight, however, is that while I learned so much from within the books that weighed me down, I learned so much more from my teachers, my friends, and my family about what I was becoming. I want to spend a few final pages relaying to you some sense of what I think will be important in these coming years as law students, and in the years that follow as lawyers.

I write to you about courage.

Let's think about what a lawyer does, and we might get a better idea of what I am talking about. Frequently the lawyer must embody the courage that her client might not be able to muster. The client comes to you and has a need or a problem. Why does the client seek out a lawyer? Because for some reason, she cannot do what the lawyer can do. Your client does not have the knowledge, the experience, or the training to do what you do. The client may need an advocate, a problem solver, or an advisor. That might require standing up in a courtroom, or it might involve sitting down at a negotiating table. Above all, it does mean taking the client, gaining her confidence, and confirming that the faith she placed in you was not mislaid.

But it is more than that. We are training you for a life after law school. And success in that life will require much courage. What is this courage that is necessary as a lawyer? It is not simply the courage of advocacy which I just mentioned. But it is the courage in deciding what to do with yourself and your education. Find a way to be courageous within yourself and your professional life. This is a noble profession, but there are too many who disrespect it, by abusing a client's trust, acting unscrupulously in court, etc., and the profession, our clients, and society all suffer for it. We must find the courage to protect our profession and the law by looking inwardly all the time and acting with courage in our lives as lawyers.

So how can we be courageous as lawyers?

Have the courage to *take a risk* for a client. Take a client with a dream for a company and help that client grow that company. Take a client who has a problem that the law has never addressed. Or, take a client who says he or she has suffered at the hands of the powerful, but who cannot afford to pay you a big fee. Have the courage *not* to say: when you have the money, come back and see me.

How else do we show courage as lawyers? Have the courage to *take on a cause* which may be unpopular. It is always easy to take on a case or a client who is popular, or well-known. You will have plenty of routine cases and transactions that will be relatively free from controversy. But you should also have the courage to take on the case that will challenge—that will keep you up nights because the struggle you represent is so large. Don't simply watch the world go by and accept the status quo. Have the courage to try to find ways to change the law for the better. To paraphrase Robert F. Kennedy, Sr., don't simply see things as they are and ask why, but imagine that which is not and ask why not?

Thurgood Marshall and Jack Greenberg exemplify this attitude. Most know Thurgood Marshall as a U.S. Supreme Court Justice, but there was much more to him than that. His legacy may be greater as a litigator than as a Justice. Before Marshall was appointed to the nation's highest court, he was a practicing lawyer of extraordinary courage. He led a team of lawyers in the fight to desegregate this nation. This was not a popular endeavor. It would have been far easier for him to accept the state of the law and continue to live in an America legally divided by race. But he had the courage to try to change the law in a dramatic way. And we are all better for that.

And who was Jack Greenberg? He was a white man, a lawyer, who spearheaded the effort against discrimination with Thurgood Marshall, hand in hand, side by side. He risked so much by taking on such an unpopular cause. But Greenberg had learned the lesson found in the words of a Protestant Minister, Martin Niemoller, who lived in Nazi Germany. Niemoller said:

> In Germany they came first for the communists, and I didn't speak up because I wasn't a communist. Then they came for the Jews, and I didn't speak up because I wasn't a Jew. Then they came for the trade unionists, and I didn't speak up because I wasn't a trade unionist. Then they came for the Catholics, and I didn't speak up because I was a protestant. Then they came for *me*, and by that time no one was left to speak up.

Jack Greenberg lived these words. He showed the courage to stand up against the kind of bigotry that robs us all of our personal freedom. You, too, have and can show such courage.

How else do we show our courage as members of this noble profession? Have the courage to keep an open mind about your future job as a lawyer: work in government, go into business, even become a law professor! In coming to law school, you made a very big decision to commit yourself to a profession—the legal profession.

But you did not choose *a job*. Yes, most of you will be practicing lawyers. Or you can set your sights on public service as a judge. Maybe in-house counsel. Or maybe take the path of Nelson Mandela, baseball manager Tony LaRussa, or artist Henri Matisse, all of whom studied law. Whatever the case may be, if the spirit so moves you, maintain the courage *not to* practice, but you will always be pleasantly surprised at how well your legal training serves you.

So what does all of that have to do with you, here, now, in the beginning of law school? As you embark on this important journey, I want to help prepare you for the tasks ahead. Besides getting the courage needed once you are finished with law school, it also will take much courage to get *through* law school. I remember how I felt—the feeling in my stomach—on the day I started law school, and I applaud the courage that you displayed simply by beginning your first year of law school. But you will need courage in so many ways to get you through.

How can you be courageous as law students? Let me suggest a few answers.

First, have the courage to speak in class, particularly when you are not sure how your answer will be received. Every day you will be faced with an array of subjects—Con Law, Contracts, Civ Pro, Torts, etc. You will sit in the classroom. Wondering what will happen. Waiting for that moment when you are called on.

Many of you will try the various techniques honed by generations of 1L's before you, to avoid being called upon by the professor:

- *The Slump Down*—where you slump down in your seat, hoping to disappear in the folds of the seat, or at least out of the view of the professor.

- *The Look Down*—you will look down to ensure that the professor does not make eye contact and call on you.
- *The Stare Down*—you look straight at the professor, almost daring the professor to call on you, but truly hoping that the professor will search for a less (apparently) willing participant.

But when that client comes to you, depending upon you to have courage, what do you think your client wants—the Slump Down champ or someone with the courage to think hard and talk straight?

But even more than simply the courage to speak when called upon, you need another kind of courage. Have the courage *to volunteer*; raise your hand and speak up, even when you are not sure that your answer is "good" or "right". We are in the business of ideas, and we must be willing to try them out to see how they work. We learn by speaking out with care and courage, to see how our ideas will be received. Some will be praised. Others will be criticized. We must learn from both experiences, and we must gather our courage to speak when we are unsure what reaction awaits our words.

How else do you need courage as a law student? Have the courage not to judge harshly the person who displays the courage to put herself out there and express her ideas. Sometimes you will disagree with your classmates or professors. Fine. When someone speaks, listen; then analyze the idea. Challenge it, even criticize it. But have the courage not to brand *the person*. Treat the person with whom you disagree with civility and kindness. Be courageous not to engage in a personal, ad hominem attack on the individual who has spoken.

Let me suggest one other way to be courageous in law school. Have the courage, in the midst of all the hard work, to keep your perspective. You may have heard horror stories about how law school is so hard, or perhaps you watched *The Paper Chase* or read the book *One L*. I will not lie to you and tell you that law school is easy. You will work hard, maybe harder than ever before. But have the courage to keep your perspective.

Remember: law school can be enjoyable. Have the courage to make it so. Don't surrender to the unfortunately too-often real pressure to be miserable. Instead, take the time to make friends among your classmates, for these folks will be your friends and professional colleagues for life. So in between the long hours of studying, enjoy yourself, your friends, your family. They are the ones who got you here, will get you through, and will be there for you when you are out of law school.

What's the point of all this?, you may be wondering. It's a reminder for you to not always take the easy path. You face a few years of classes, reading assignments, and exams. Then you will be faced with decades of a career in the law. It is too easy simply to let each day go by, to accept what it has, and to do no more than what is asked of you. It is easy to go to class and go home, rather than sticking around for a debate on the death penalty or free speech. In the practice of law, it is easy to take on the same type of case over and over again—familiar territory is comforting. It is easy to avoid the difficult challenges and unpopular cases—controversy is unsettling. It is simple to focus solely on the limited task before you and to perform each task in a mechanical fashion—new challenges are hard work. It is easy to settle for the daily routine.

The challenge in being a lawyer worthy of this profession is not to do the same thing every day. Stop yourself and have the courage to ask, to challenge, to question what you see. If you are a good lawyer, important decisions should confront you every day. They do not necessarily stand up and announce themselves as life-altering decisions. But you must make the decisions. With courage. Seek out the real challenges. Make the tough choices. Have the courage to make your decisions based on more than your economic interest. Have the courage to make a decision without regard to the *un*popularity of your position. You know what you believe is right. Stand up for it. Live it.